DEVOLUTION

Essays Edited by
Harry Calvert

Professional Books Ltd.
London
1975

ISBN 0 903486 06 7

Printed in Great Britain

CONTENTS

CONTENTS

I   INTRODUCTION

This volume of essays consists of papers presented at the Annual Colloquium of the United Kingdom National Committee on Comparative Law at Cardiff in September 1974. The papers are printed virtually as presented and each, of course, represents only the views of its author. They are schematic only to the extent that certain contributors were asked to focus upon a specific jurisdiction, Bradley on Scotland, de Forges on France, Dagtoglou on Germany, Rimanque on Belgium and Williams on Wales. Otherwise, the content of the papers has been determined largely by the author's own view of what was relevant and currently important.

The Colloquium therefore was not (and nor is this volume) intended to offer a definitive assessment of the question of devolution in the United Kingdom today. It could, however, and did provoke some relevant questions, deriving largely from experience elsewhere and, in the present context of proposals for devolution in the United Kingdom, the papers may perhaps provoke some scepticism.

The British Government's White Paper (publication of which coincided with the first day of the colloquium) may perhaps be fairly described as bred by political expediency out of the Kilbrandon Report. There undoubtedly are problems of government in the United Kingdom today; the Kilbrandon Report sets out a range of views as to how they might be solved; the White Paper adds to that range. At the end of the day, I remain more dubious than before about what is now, almost inevitably, about to happen.

It is important in the first place to be clear about what the present problems of government are. Certain features, such as the felt lack of participation and communication and the sense of grievance and frustration of the people, which inform the Kilbran-

1

don study, seem to be more or less generally agreed. These vices do not, however, seem to recognise regional boundaries; they may even be said to be endemic throughout much of Western Europe and perhaps farther afield. There is a fundamental confusion here between psychological and geographical remoteness from the seat of government which I think has befuddled the whole question of devolution.

Some matters certainly do have geographical implications. Certain parts of the United Kingdom are undoubtedly the object of nationalist sentiment, particularly so far as minorities in Scotland, Wales and the South-West are concerned (and Northern Ireland, meanwhile, remains beset by a strange double nationalism). Nor can it be denied that some such regions have cultural peculiarities — Wales its language, Scotland its law most of all, but English regional cultures also. What can and should be strenuously questioned is whether there is any causal connection whatever between such national and cultural phenomena and the generalised grievances earlier mentioned and shared amongst Her Majesty's subjects at large, whether Scottish, Welsh or Geordie. If we assume that there is, then we run the danger of relying upon institutions apt to deal with one set of problems to cope with a quite different range of difficulties which, far from easing, they may exacerbate. On the one hand, the establishment of a Scottish Assembly in Edinburgh is unlikely to do much for a disaffected Kentishman in Dartford. On the other hand, genuinely nationalist feeling will be little assuaged by the adoption of a new code of manners for the civil service.

If there is no such causal connection, then it may be that we have not learned as much as we might from the continental experience some of which is described in these essays, to say nothing of reviewing, overhauling and perhaps adding to our own existing institutions.

Can we learn anything about improving the efficiency and sensitivity of the administration of central government services in the various regions from the French prefectoral system? To what extent does our present parliamentary system render Members impotent fully to protect their constituents' interests from central government because of the divided loyalties imposed by the party system; does this not argue for a massive extension of the "ombudsman" principle, however institutionalised; but, then, how likely is it that a government and governing party would be

2

persuaded to make such a bed for themselves?

Again, if there is no causal connection between the national and cultural phenomena on the one hand and generalised grievances on the other, what is a desirable constitutional response to the undoubted distinguishing cultural and national factors? Culturally, may we not learn from a closer examination of the Belgian experience? Real power to determine a narrow range of cultural matters may be a much more apt response than illusory power over a broad range of matters. And whether power is real or illusory will be to a large extent a function of independent sources of finance. Such sources might be perfectly feasible on the small scale demanded by a narrow range of cultural affairs (which, of course, assumes that not all education is included) but utterly irreconcilable with central government planning on any larger scale.

What of nationalism? In so far as it derives force from new sources of wealth alleged to be regionally "owned", have the consequences of a positive response been worked out? If so, how will the precedent be distinguished if, in a decade or two, claims are mounted on behalf of Northumbria, Yorkshire and East Anglia. In so far as nationalism derives from other sources (and to a substantial extent it does and is merely fortified in its popular support by the North Sea oil argument) what is the case for devolution as opposed to federation or separatism? The fact that separation was ruled out of the Kilbrandon Commission's remit by its terms of reference does not cause it to cease to be a constitutional question of the first importance. It may be an apt response; it at least has the merit, very doubtful in the case of the devolutionary schemes hinted at in the White Paper, of conferring substantial power upon the new states. If the demand for substantial power (which I take to mean a sufficient degree of self-determination) is there, may not some form of federalism be a much more fruitful invention than devolution, as David Williams so cogently argues in his paper. As the Northern Ireland experience seems to teach us, the establishment of institutions of devolutionary government may well be an irreversible step. If devolution does not still the demand (as seems likely with the present proposals) the direction, inevitably to be urged by those calling for more in the first place and condemning devolution as inadequate from the start, likely to be taken is towards separatism. It is surely better to get it right at the start than to follow error by crisis and that crisis by further error.

Either a sufficient degree of self-determination is a political necessity or it is not. If it is, ought we not to look more closely at the continental experience embraced by the Kilbrandon dissenters but dismissed, perhaps too lightly, by the majority. If so, we must do so with caution. Under the German system, real access to power seems to be given to *Länder* representatives via the application of the interlocking principle in the *Bundesrat*. With us, life peerages have already imperceptibly changed the character of the House of Lords and it is tempting to propose an extension of that process so as to give responsible regional representatives a real say in the determination and criticism of central government policy on regional matters. It is a temptation to which no one who has read Professor Dagtoglou's essays will lightly succumb, although he need not be completely deterred.

I can appreciate the impatience with which one who urges reconsideration is likely to be received in some quarters. The problems are, after all, by no means recent or novel and delaying decisions imposes no moratorium on grievances. The unfortunate fact is that the wrong answers to the questions that have heretofore been asked will not do so either.

To me, the papers herein prompt many questions. Their significance is that they prompt some questions different from those that have heretofore been asked. He who cries "Enough of these questions, let's have some answers" misses this point and does an injustice to the Kilbrandon Commission and those many authors who ventured into this field previously. There can be no doubt that there is a risk of strictly irrelevant considerations bastardising decisions which are about to be made. It is surely no mere coincidence that the Labour and Conservative Parties have come to take devolution seriously just at the point in history when Nationalist parties have started to pose a serious electoral threat. There may be a good constitutional argument for retaining 71 Scottish seats (whilst keeping Ulster pegged at 12) at Westminster, but it also happens to be the case that a diminution in their number would impose an electoral handicap. The latest proposals may be good or not. But at least we should be sure that they are not yet another example of that recently more common phenomenon, the unworkable British compromise.

Blades, 18 January 1975   HC

4

II   DEVOLUTION IN PERSPECTIVE

Harry Calvert *

Previously regarded as a lunatic fringe phenomenon, nationalism in Scotland and Wales suddenly seemed to be becoming a serious feature of the electoral scene when, at the time of the 1966
general election, a fifth of the electorate in those countries gave it
their primary loyalty. This prompted the Labour government of
the day, perhaps not entirely unmindful of the fact that the
Labour Party had more of the Scottish and Welsh seats to lose
than anyone else, to appoint a Royal Commission, under the
chairmanship first of Lord Crowther and then of Lord Kilbrandon, to inquire into the need for constitutional change. The
Report which emerged from their deliberations, the most valuable contribution to the literature on our constitution in recent
years, recommends change in the direction of more devolution of
government on a regional basis.

Pragmatically, the power of government needs always to be distributed among a number of individuals if the business of government is to be carried on. Even the despot will need to vest
authority in others if his position is to be sustained; he cannot personally collect all the taxes, punish all the criminals and, single-
handed, wage a foreign war. In all but the very smallest and sim-
plest of polities, then, authority needs to be distributed among a
number of persons.

Regional devolution is a type of such distribution; but it is just
one type of many It does not necessarily follow, because some
redistribution of authority is needed, that regional devolution is
the best way. The purpose of this paper is first to set out the range
of ways in which authority can be distributed and then, briefly,
to consider which methods of redistribution may be thought to

Professor of Law, University of Newcastle upon Tyne.

be most apt as responses to the various current pressures.

Modes of distributing authority may be conveniently classified into the following:

A. Modes of distribution within the centre;
B. "Vertical" distribution, i.e. modes of distribution involving the vesting of authority in entities outside the centre and exercising authority on a broad front by reference to some territorial unit such as a locality or a region;
C. "Horizontal" distribution, i.e. the distribution of authority in respect of a particular function or functions of government to an entity outside the centre without territorial limitation but by reference to function, e.g. British Rail.

Before discussing these modes in greater detail, two preliminary points must be made. Firstly, these various modes are not mutually exclusive but can and, indeed, almost invariably are, combined — strictly speaking, they are dimensions of distribution. Secondly, there exists another dimension of the distribution of authority to which further reference will be made later. "Authority" in relation to a particular region or function, is complex and divisible. The choice is not simply between distributing all or no authority in relation to a particular matter. Authority may be distributed in relation to one role of government but not others — thus administration may be devolved, but not legislation, in relation to a particular matter.

A. Modes of Distribution within the Centre

The extremes of the scale here are, on the one hand anarchy, and on the other hand the vesting of total authority in a single individual. Every modern state in fact engages in a very extensive distribution of authority amongst various agencies within the centre whilst none embraces anarchy.

In speaking of "authority" here, I am not talking about ultimate overriding authority, but about all manifestations of it, including subordinate authority. The doctrine of the separation of powers lauds the advisability of distributing ultimate authority among different entities, none of which is subject to control by the others within its sphere, such sphere, however, being limited. Such distribution is not, however, the only type possible within the centre. In the United Kingdom, for example, judges adjudicate, but so, also, do Ministers of the Crown. Cabinets, ministers, department heads and even inferior officials from policy

6

and the last three actually execute various decisions, sometimes their own, sometimes those of others. Parliament (within which authority is distributed amongst the Crown and the two Houses, within each of which it is further distributed among members, groups of members and officials) certainly, but also Ministers, civil servants and draftsmen, legislate, all this notwithstanding Parliamentary supremacy. And, still within the centre, some control over the exercise of power by others is asserted by institutions such as the Comptroller and Auditor General, the Parliamentary Commissioner for Administration, Committees of the Houses, the Council on Tribunals, ad hoc investigations etc., as well as by the Houses themselves, and internal checks by those exercising the authority.

Central government authority may, in fact, be vested in entities or individuals physically located in particular localities or regions and authorised to act in relation to such localities or regions, e.g. central government services may be locally administered. The Kilbrandon Report and Memorandum of Dissent both cite such instances as illustrating the existing extent of "devolution" within the United Kingdom. It is, however, important to distinguish "devolution" in this sense from "devolution" as described below. Terms such as "the centre" and "remoteness" are ambiguous and there is a danger of confusing conceptual centrality with geographical location and psychological remoteness with physical remoteness. Much of our regional administration exemplifies the continental "deconcentration". Devolution is normally thought of as a species of "decentralisation".

B. Vertical Distribution

The hall-mark of the vertical distribution of power is its attachment to territorial limits, such as the parish, the locality, the region, province or country and, of course, the state itself. That functions of government should be discharged more or less comprehensively by reference to territory in this way seems to go without question. Perhaps it should be questioned. The reasons may be found in any of psychology, social psychology, communications, defence, ease of administration, history and others. It should be questioned if only to be sure that it is a sound basis for government to the extent that it forms such a basis. The horizontal distribution of power (e.g. as to a public corporation charged with the mining and marketing of coal) is, after all, an increas-

ingly common phenomenon, whilst nomadic polities, personal
laws and condominia are not unknown.

Vertical distribution remains, however, common. It takes
many forms:

(a) It may be distributed "upwards" by confederation, as in the
case of the E.E.C. Federation upwards may, of course, take
place but will involve the reconstruction of the federating
state and the consequent redefinition of modes of distribution of power within the reconstructed state.

(b) It may be distributed "downwards". Federation and separation are analogous to confederation and federation
"upwards", separation involving the reconstruction of
states. The usually accepted criterion of federalism is divided
sovereignty, neither centre nor member states possessing the
totality of authority ultimately. This is, however, a legal criterion. In terms of actual functioning, a predominance of
actual power in the member states may render a federation
indistinguishable from a confederation; similarly, a predominance of actual power in the centre may render a federation indistinguishable from some varieties of the unitary
state with devolution. In speaking of "predominance" here,
aspects of public finance, and particularly the power to tap
the chief sources of revenue, loom large.

(c) All other modes of vertical distribution of authority must
exist within the unitary state, i.e. the state within which sovereignty is undivided and located wholly in the centre (though
a rigid constitution may demand a careful definition of "the
centre"). "Sovereignty" however, means ultimate legal
authority, and the concentration of this ultimate power in
the centre does not preclude the distribution, vertically or horizontally, of subordinate authority. Vertically, there is no logical limit to the number of territorial units chosen or to the
number of "levels" on which authority may be distributed.
The legal history of the British Islands has witnessed the vesting of authority in thousands of territorial units at all levels
from the largest counties or regions to the parish or immediate locality. Historically, extensive governmental functions
have long been discharged by local authorities of various
kinds for many centuries and a re-vamped form of local government now contains the lowest "levels" among which
authority is distributed within the United Kingdom. It is to
the distribution of authority to intermediate levels, between

central and local government that the term "devolution" is normally applied in English-speaking jurisdictions.

The criterion for devolutionary systems — that they employ modes of distribution of authority within a unitary state with a sovereign centre — is again a legal one. The shape of government and the actual distribution of power in practice may vary according to other factors, among which two in particular deserve mention. The first again relates to the question of public finance and in particular the disposition of the power to tap the major sources of revenue to carry with it centripetal or centrifugal tendencies according as to whether it is located in the centre or at the intermediate level respectively. Thus, if too much power is actually vested in the intermediate institutions there may be a tendency to resemble federation; whilst if too much power resides in the centre, devolution may become illusory, and virtually indistinguishable from the regional administration of central government services.

The second factor above-mentioned is the tendency of institutions once established, to perpetuate themselves, if possible to grow, and at least to become jealous of their power. Much of the evidence in favour of an extension of devolution presented to the Kilbrandon Commission came from local and regional politicians and officials; no evidence from this source argued for any contraction of devolution. Similarly, by the 1960s, Northern Ireland politicians of the same ilk as that which had, in the 1920s, resisted the imposition of a devolutionary system, had come to vigorously asserting a total lack of any authority in the centre to "trespass" in Northern Ireland's "internal affairs".

On devolution in general, two further points should be mentioned. First, within the United Kingdom, devolution today is normally thought of as involving the delegation of authority from the centre, or decentralisation. It should be noted that a state of devolution can be arrived at in whole or in part in other ways. It can, and within the United Kingdom to some extent has, come about not only by delegation from the centre but also by concentration from the local level. Joint police authorities are one example. Indeed, a comparison of local government itself in the United Kingdom in the "horse-and-buggy" days and now, in the "jet" age reveals a marked advance in the direction of devolution as part of a larger historical process in which some governmental functions gravitate "upwards" from localities to reside ultimately in the centre, social security being an example. Furthermore, it is perfectly possible in principle (and in some African states is the case in practice) for a state of devolution to be arrived at autochthonously and to have been received into the constitutional structure of a new state simply by derivation from the pre-existing social organisation.

The second further point to make is that it may be unhelpful to think of devolution (or any other mode of distribution of authority) as a settled state of things. Much that is written on devolution seems to view it in static rather than dynamic terms. It may be helpful always to bear in mind that devolution can be viewed as a process as well as a product. Problems of social and political organisation change over time; so, therefore, will the aptness of particular solutions offered. One vice in the Stormont-type devolution enjoyed by Northern Ireland for 50 years related to exactly this point. What by 1970 had come to be regarded as essential democratic safeguards simply were not thought of as such at all in 1920.

C. Horizontal Devolution

As is stated above, this means distributing authority by reference to function rather than territory. Within the centre, such functional distribution forms the raison d'être of departments of state, ministries and branches. Outside the centre, the vesting of power in relation to a particular function such as postal services, transport, exploitation of mineral resources, in some entity such as a public corporation is common. Considerable reliance may be placed, however, on private entities even in relation to such a fundamental governmental function as national defence.

Mention has so far been made of three modes of distribution of authority — A. Within the centre; B. Vertical; and C. Horizontal. It is convenient, now, to advert to the other dimension of distribution of authority, for the existence of this further dimension offers us a range of different models of devolution. This further dimension is the fact that in relation to any aspect of social life, government may involve not one but several activities, authority to engage in all or any of which may be devolved. Thus policies may be discussed, formulated and proposed; policy-decisions or choices may be made; legislation may be necessary in which case drafting, debate, amendment, enactment and promulgation must take place. Laws will need to be executed and schemes administered. Disputes may arise and provision for their pacific

10

or, if necessary, forceful settlement may need to be made. Furthermore, wherever a limited authority to do all or any of these things is conferred, there arises the possibility of abuse of that power and hence of devices designed to curb such abuse, an entirely separate and, in many countries, a highly valued function of government. A devolutionary system may therefore be invested, in relation to one or more aspects of social life, with one or more (including all) these functions of government, the range, whether vertically or horizontally, thus extending from purely consultative or advisory functions in relation to minor matters on the one hand to plenary powers on the other.

This, then, is the range of devices for the distribution of authority available to us as a response to certain pressures. We may employ all, any or none of them. It remains to consider the implications of those pressures.

The Pressures for Change

Many different streams of opinion contribute to the flow which carries towards devolution and many of these now seem influential in the United Kingdom. If one examines major sources, such as the Kilbrandon papers, the White Papers on Northern Ireland, and a host of more or less learned articles and newspaper comments, one may detect at least six different influences. As will be seen, even some of these six are complex. And if one takes a wider view it will be seen that historically and comparatively, devolution has stemmed from other sources, e.g. the desire of a conquering state to disperse power within the previously powerfully-centred conquered state, thus preventing strong nationalism re-emerging.

Before proceeding to analyse current influences and considering how, in their light, we should view devolution, two preliminary points must be made. (1) The truth about alleged social pressures may be very hard to establish. A pressure does not exist merely because it is alleged to exist; nor will it necessarily be what it is alleged to be. Identification of and a proper appreciation of such forces as there are is an immense evidentiary problem. People will not always say what they mean; they will not necessarily even know what they mean; and even if they do, it will not necessarily make sense. (2) There is a tendency today to think of devolution as a panacea; to assume that the current pressures tend happily in the same direction and that a single model scheme

11

will accommodate them all — it is merely a problem of working out the most apt scheme. This may not be so at all; what contains one pressure may fortify another. Experience in Northern Ireland may be teaching us this at this very moment. Certainly, one view of current constitutional developments there is that whereas a cleaned-up, fairer, version of the 1920 scheme should have worked well in Northern Ireland had the mass of the population favoured retaining the union with Great Britain, it cannot do so now because the unity of the state itself is seriously questioned. We turn now to the various pressures.

(i) *National, cultural, ethnic and socio-historical pressures*

These factors have in common that they are essentially socio-psychological (though they are commonly associated with other real or imagined influences such as economic betterment). They are not, however, by any means identical, though they may co-exist. They do raise a number of issues which should be resolved before any decisions are made.

(a) How real and extensive are these various and different pressures? The Attitudes Survey commissioned by Kilbrandon, which is considered later (*post*, pp.41-62), suggests that in many respects Scotland and particularly Wales are virtually indistinguishable from some regions of England in relation to which nationalist claims are never voiced. This prompts one to ask whether what are voiced as nationalist claims may not be, in substance, claims in title of cultures; and this is crucial, not only because equality of citizenship requires equal regard for all cultures. It is crucial also because institutions which are apt to accommodate nationalist pressures may be totally inapt to accommodate cultural pressures and vice versa.

(b) If the pressures are truly nationalist, is devolution an apt response at all? Nationalists, after all, tell us it is not what they want although they are, like the rest of us, ready to settle for half a loaf now and the other half later. The point is that devolution may not solve anything at all; it may simply fuel nationalism. Its inaptness is the burden of Mansergh's caveat against "supposing that it (devolution) is a means of satisfying nationalist claims. It is not" he tells us. "It suggests only a means whereby better government may be secured within a single state. Its value disappears once the unity of the state is questioned." *(The Government of Northern Ireland, p.16).*

(c) What considerations then should govern the response to nationalist and such like claims? Another lesson taught us by Northern Ireland is that any constitutional device has to meet two conditions: (1) it has to satisfy the aspirations of some *and* (2) it has to enjoy at least the acquiescence of virtually all the rest. Indeed, one might argue that whilst (1) is a desirable condition only, (2) is actually a necessary one. The corollary might be that a nationalist minority should have its way; or that a nationalist majority should not; or even that devolution might be an apt response to other influences prevailing amongst a particular group, nationalist claims notwithstanding.

(ii) *The need to extend real participation in democratic processes*

Again, many questions need to be answered. When one talks about participation what, precisely, does one mean? Does one mean that many more people should have the opportunity to play a part in all aspects of the governmental function? I doubt if this is so. There is at present no bar whatever to the private individual contemplating and proposing policies — the correspondence columns of the press are full of it. I know of no great or deeply felt popular demand to participate in the legislative process; and there sometimes seems even to be a negative demand to participate in law enforcement. If participation in all aspects of government is not urged, then in which aspect or aspects is it urged? The Kilbrandon Attitudes Survey, to be considered later, gives us some clues. The common complaints are about a "lack of democracy", about "central government being insensitive", about "alienation from the processes of government". One is pushed in the direction of concluding that the aspect of government which is uppermost in the minds of those who feel "powerless" when confronted by a "faceless bureaucracy" is the prevention of abuse of power by effective control of the administration.

Is there anything novel about this? There is a good argument that there is nothing novel about it all, that for years and years we have simply mistaken the form for the substance of social democracy at all events as described, for example, in Benn & Peters, *Social Principles of the Democratic State.* If this is so, then it is

13

not the phenomenon of an overbearing political and administrative system that is novel but rather the extent of popular appreciation of that fact.

However one answers these questions, what reason is there to suppose that devolution offers a solution? In what way would devolutionary government be, or, indeed, is local government, more democratic, more sensitive, less overbearing? In what way would or does it heighten the sense of participation. Westminster may indeed be much more remote, geographically, than the town hall but does this matter at all? Are M.P.s less accessible than local councillors are, or than regional representatives would be? and even if they are, why are they? There is presently some confusion between local and central government responsibility (there used to be even more in Northern Ireland where the man in the street's knowledge of the distinction between transferred and excepted matters lacked sophistication). Would an extension of the responsibilities of the intermediate level help? If it is simply that M.P.s are overburdened, an increase in their number or in the scope of horizontal devolution might be equally, or even more, apt.

If one assumes for purposes of argument that there is closer contact on the local and would be closer contract on an intermediate level, even so, effective participation would remain a function of power, and unless the new institutions were vested with real power, hopes of a greater sensitivity would be frustrated. Immediately after 1920, Northern Ireland had to choose and preferred sufficiency in chains to autonomy in poverty. This might not matter for a prosperous region but in the poorer regions (from which the main cry for devolution seems to stem) there might be very little effective participation unless new devices, particularly in relation to public financing, were contrived. Here, as elsewhere, questions of public finance occupy the centre of the stage.

If one assumes both closer contact *and* power to do something in consequence, then a case may be made out for vertical devolution. It might indeed offer the possibility of a local or regional majority controlling things notwithstanding that in the state as a whole they might be doomed to minority status. Even so, it is legitimate to ask whether this might not, in fact, be a good several times removed. Vertical devolution might be a passably efficient vehicle, but it might be far from the best vehicle. A different approach might yield different results. What is it that the people want to participate in? In relation to what matters do complaints of insensitivity most commonly occur? The areas of greatest grievance so far as the P.C.A. is concerned are areas likely to remain with the centre under most devolutionary schemes so far proposed. Many other areas of grievance, e.g. in relation to postal services, transport, health services etc., are already subject to devolution of a horizontal or hybrid type. Perhaps what we need is a greater infusion of democratic processes into horizontal devolution and more effective safeguards against abuse at the centre. It is far from self-evident that vertical devolution is the obvious response. There is here a great danger of confusion arising from the ambiguities in such concepts as "remoteness".

(iii)   *The need for government to seem to take proper note of the needs and problems of particular groups*

(ii) above focusses upon a particular means (greater popular participation and control) of government, assuming it will lead to a desirable end, whereas (iii) focusses upon that end itself. The end itself could, in principle, be achieved by central, regional or local benevolent dictators or, more realistically, by more intensive concentration on the ground, in the regions, of the administration of central government services.

To some extent, we already have this, e.g. in local offices dealing with employment and social security, and in regional administrative structures in the same areas. Obviously, in such areas, there is a strong case for it (many local government services fall into the same category for the same reasons). The question is whether these practices should be extended; if so, via a species of devolution; and, if so, via what species? It has certainly been cogently argued (by Lawrence, *The Government of Northern Ireland*) that in some areas benefits accrued to Northern Ireland from the devolutionary system there which probably would not have accrued if government exclusively from Westminster had been continued. The eradication of tuberculosis and the awareness of local needs so far as industrial development is concerned are examples. It may nevertheless be asked whether territory at all, and in particular a specific territory for all purposes, should figure as relevant concepts in this connection. If the aim is that government should *seem* to be sensitive to the needs of particular groups, is it necessary that it be a government exclusively *of* the particular group? Wales has county option as to Sunday opening, facilitated not by a Welsh but by a Westminster Parliament.

15

Would the same facility granted by a Welsh Parliament seem to evidence greater sensitivity and if so why?

Perhaps one answer to this question lies in the principle, apparently common to Bentham and the Kilbrandon Memorandum of Dissent, that the individual should be allowed to govern himself to the greatest extent possible, with its implication that powers should be vested in authorities at the lowest possible level. This, however, argues as much against as for a single intermediate level. It argues in the direction of confining power to the group concerned, however small; and the snag here is that the group in question (e.g. comparative lawyers) may have no territorial association at all. Even if it does (e.g. the area defined by reference to journeys to work for an urban population; the "drainage basin" of a hospital) the area may well (and if the structure of existing regional organisation in the United Kingdom is any indication, does) vary with the group. There is therefore likely to be an arbitrariness about fixing upon any single territorial unit.

It is, no doubt, a sensible approach to list various functions of government in relation to which power might be more widely distributed, to identify the groups to whom power might be transferred, to examine the extent to which the groups have a particular territorial association. The result may be to steer us towards a mixture of multi-level vertical devolution and horizontal devolution, combined with a more sensitive responsibility at the centre. What is clear is that there is no logical reason why the scheme of distribution of power determined by reference to factor (iii) should coincide, even imperfectly, with that determined by reference to factor (ii).

(iv) *The need for government actually to take proper note of the needs and problems of particular groups*

Whereas factor (iii) focusses upon patent sensitivity of administration, and (ii) upon participation in it as a means of securing that end, (iv) is concerned simply with efficiency of administration, regardless of popular participation in it or the obvious sensitivity of it. It by no means follows that institutions controlled by the group affected and obviously concerned with that group's interests will be best placed to secure them effectively.

Take the question of industrial development in a particular region. It may well be that the best way to find out about the problems, to be seen to be concerned about the solution and to take

16

note of regional opinion in their solution is to have the administration on the spot. It does not at all follow that the best institutions for dealing with all problems of industrial development in a region are regional institutions. It may well be that some aspects of government would be best concentrated at the centre.

Various regions of the United Kingdom have suffered greatly from economic depression; one thinks of the 1930s and Wales, the North-East, Scotland and Northern Ireland. If it be accepted as a state objective that the better off should help the less well off within the United Kingdom, the problem is how best to achieve it. In Scotland and Wales, economic deprivation has to some extent fuelled the nationalist movements. If we take their extreme manifestation, separatism, we must contemplate two possibilities:

1. The resources of these particular regions are inadequate for self-help. Improvement can only come from the redistribution of wealth within the U.K. as a whole. If this is so, then separatism is a wholly inapt response whilst lesser variants of it, such as a federal solution or legislative devolution are neutral so far as a direct solution of problems is concerned.
2. The resources of these particular regions would, in fact, be adequate for self-help if only they were not pillaged by the U.K. as a whole. In this case, separatism is a wholly rational response and federalism and legislative devolution partly rational.

This leads us surely to see the problem, so far as (iv) is concerned, as being not so much how to vest in a region greater control over its own affairs as how to improve communication with the centre and other regions, so as to fortify sympathy with redistribution, and how best to ensure action by the centre so as effectively to realise the sympathy. The problem is surely one of ensuring responsibility and sensitivity to differing needs in the centre.

The sort of constitutional machinery which comes to mind to this end is not devolution or federalism or separatism at all, no matter how apt these might be for other purposes, but, for example, the reconstruction of the Upper House at Westminster so as to provide for regional representation, perhaps on an interlocking basis, so as to give regions a more effective say in the formulation and implementation of central government policies. Delegation of greater powers to civil servants stationed in the regions might also help. A stronger variety of hybrid devolution to regional development councils might have greater relevance than simple vertical devolution.

This is not to say that vertical devolution is totally irrelevant. It is not necessary for the centre to make and execute all regional development decisions. It is merely to say that there are limits to the extent to which regional institutions can assist a particular region in relation to some functions of government. It might be appropriate for regional institutions, rather than regional outposts of the central administration, to oversee the actual location of industries in the particular region; and there might be another role, that of actual liaison with the centre as to the size of the slice of the national cake which ought to be offered to the region, the role of the regional institutions being to inform the centre of matters which might otherwise be overlooked. Both these roles were efficiently discharged by the devolved institutions in Northern Ireland. The fact that there might be such roles should not, however, blind us to the obvious fact that they are subsidiary roles and that in so far as actually dealing with regional poverty costs money, and requires national redistribution, the main problem is that of increasing awareness and sensitivity in the centre. Nor should we fall into the error of assuming that vertically devolved institutions are uniquely suitable for the discharge even of these subsidiary roles.

(v) *The need to relieve central government of some of its burdens*

It was, so far as I am aware, Thomas Jefferson who coined the term "devolution", proposing "to lighten the cares of the central legislature by judicious devolution". If too much is demanded of central institutions, either the individuals who man them will be unduly burdened; or the work will be done in a manner which from one point of view or another will be regarded as unsatisfactory. If one looks at the burdens which, for example, the Westminster institutions are called upon to bear it is obvious that if their organisation and procedures had not been very considerably modified over the years, they simply could not have borne all the burdens efficiently. This state of affairs is the original, Jeffersonian, justification for devolution.

It is, superficially, a sufficient justification. But Parliament and the Executive have of course, modified their behaviour very considerably over the years and further modification along these lines is obviously a possible alternative. In other words, although it is true that if you can't do it all yourself you must delegate, it does not follow that you must delegate to a particular person or institution outside the centre, let alone to newly created regional institutions. There is, already, a great deal of delegation. The bulk of our legislation is now "delegated". Much of the work which the House of Commons formerly did itself it now delegates to committees, standing and otherwise. Most Parliamentary questions and answers are now written; members usually do not attend; even prayers have been curtailed. Much of Parliament's less controversial work is now, in effect, delegated to the House of Lords. A great deal of central government activity is "delegated" to public corporations which are, in substance, semi-autonomous. We have recently seen yet other government functions "delegated", i.e. hived-off to private enterprise. Even the Cabinet seems to work in committees to a much greater extent than formerly, with consequential modifications of collective responsibility.

If either the Westminster institutions are now so overburdened that there is no longer any capacity for expansion; or if delegation within the centre is, for some reason, unsatisfactory, then some other solution to the problem of relieving the centre must be found, though even then it does not follow that it must be found in the relatively new and untried way of creating new regional institutions.

In deciding what approach to adopt to this problem, it is perhaps a good idea to probe rather more deeply into what we mean when we talk about Parliament etc. being overburdened, before we start conceiving of the means of relief. The fact is that Parliament's work is various, but all time-consuming. To the extent that pressure on Parliamentary time has meant the delegation of much legislative power to the administration, perhaps we should be examining ways and means of ensuring a greater and more confidence-inspiring responsibility of the administration. Traditionally, one looks to the House of Commons for that, but this is the second major respect in which the House has become overburdened and inefficient. We do have ancillary machinery, such as the Parliamentary Commissioner for Administration, which could surely be made much more effective; and such as the courts, which seem to persist in ignoring the fact that powers delegated by Parliament to administrative agencies are usually vague and never have precise "boundaries" beyond which it is forbidden for the administrator to "trespass". To the extent that over-burden-ing means that insufficient attention is paid to the roles which the House of Commons retains for itself, there may be a role for some form of devolution. Few bills nowadays receive exhaustive attention and when they are Scottish or Welsh bills it is easy to see the appeal of the argument that a Scottish or Welsh legislature would do the job better, the committee system notwithstanding. Even here, however, there may be scope for improving regional participation in the Westminster processes (as, for example, by greatly extended regional representation in the House of Lords); and, in any case, Scottish and Welsh bills are not the only scantily treated ones — indeed, the special provision presently made for them may well mean that they have fewer grievances than the English regions.

Even if one decides to devolve, again one might ask whether simple vertical devolution is necessarily the right response. It may well be, again, that the hybrid model, e.g. regional educational councils, is just as, if not more apt.

(vi) *Implementing policies effecting a different distribution of wealth as amongst various groups*

A catalogue of motivations towards devolution would not, nowadays, be complete without reference to this factor. We have, of course, always had rich and poor regions in the sense that the official figures of incomes per head in various regions vary. It has always been open to a rich region to argue that some species of home-rule would ensure to its advantage simply by enabling it to retain more of or all of the wealth it produces for its own benefit, i.e. repudiate the obligation to improve the lot of the less well off. This type of argument is now being articulated and appears to have gained some popular appeal in Scotland recently due to the promise of economic betterment held out by North Sea oil. A variant of this argument (and a fairer paraphrase of the current Scottish argument?) is that some species of home-rule would be the most effective check against pillaging by the rest of the United Kingdom.

Either way, it is a compelling argument viewed from the standpoint of a region which is, actually, better-endowed than the rest. But it can hardly be expected to appeal to other, poorer, regions. When Terence O'Neill, later to become Prime Minister of Northern Ireland (and now Lord O'Neill of the Mayne), youthfully enamoured of devolution, publicly expressed a desire to see it extended to other parts of the United Kingdom, he was sternly reminded by a more seasoned colleague that no sensible Ulsterman wanted too many calves sucking at that particular cow. He meant, of course, that there was a finite amount of milk and that it was insufficient for Ulster-sized shares all round; but the arithmetic is the same if, as a result of devolution all round, the fatter calves take more.

There is another reason why this justification can be expected to lack popular appeal. It imperils the unity of the state as a whole. This is clearly so in so far as separatism is the logical conclusion of such thinking; but it is equally so to the extent that first priority is given to the regional group, for the interests of that group and the state as a whole will inevitably conflict. It is, of course, a matter of what arrangement of things can enjoy the acquiescence of people generally; but the range of real choices available rarely includes the ideal and if one wants the benefits of membership of the larger state one is likely to be asked to pick up one's share of the burdens (Northern Ireland's current dilemma). Some of those benefits may well be, on grounds of scale (e.g. national defence; domestic markets), peculiar to the larger state.

Summary

A very common way of approaching questions of devolution is to ask, firstly, should we devolve or not, and secondly, what type of devolution should we have? That was the governmental thinking which inspired the establishment of the Crowther (later Kilbrandon) Commission (in so far as it was not more cynically motivated); that was the way the Commission itself, dissenters excepted, chose to read its remit. The burden of this paper has been to argue for a somewhat different approach. Devolution, of which there are many variants, is simply one of a number of medicines which might be administered to cure our ills; there is nothing in the nature of devolution itself to suggest that it is the appropriate medicine, any more than antibiotics are, in themselves, the appropriate medicine. One needs to know something about the illness; and I have tried to suggest that the symptons described by the patient are not homogeneous but, on the contrary, heterogeneous, in so far as they are not obscure. We ought therefore to be very wary about making the assumption that there is one medicine which will restore almost complete health to the body politic, let alone that that medicine is regional government of a particular type.

It seems to me that of the various tasks which have to be undertaken, a few can be singled out as being of particular importance:

1. Diagnosis of the illness — what, exactly, are our actual current ills. The Kilbrandon Commission took this question very seriously and made a brave attempt to answer it. This will be separately dealt with (*post* pp. 41-62).

2. Evolution of criteria which will determine what functions are apt for devolution, either horizontal or vertical, and of the aspects of government in relation to those functions which are so apt.

3. In so far as investing devolved institutions with real power is essential to cure of the ills, how can this be effected; in particular, what financial arrangements can best reconcile the pulls of centre and devolved institutions?

III THE KILBRANDON REPORT : SOME COMMENTS*
Terence Daintith†

Few Royal Commissions have had as rough a passage as the Commission on the Constitution. The voyage was dogged by misfortune — two deaths among the crew, three more jumped ship — and disagreement — not only two outright mutineers, but dissension among the remainder as to which of five possible courses to follow; and the welcome, when the weary crew paddled into port with their heavy cargo after four long years at sea, had a fair part of derision in it. They deserved better, and when the people showed unequivocally that they were attracted by the new constitutional wares the Commission brought back with them, they got it. What had once been viewed gloomily as a twentieth-century Darien expedition was suddenly recognised as the first exploration of an exciting new land of constitutional change and development, whose confines and topography are now being exhaustively plotted by governmental working parties.

With these later developments, whose outcome is still, at the time of writing, unpredictable, it is not my purpose to deal. This paper rather looks back to the Kilbrandon Report, with a view to expounding its contents in a short compass and demonstrating what seem, to one public lawyer, to be the principal implications and problems of the main streams of thought within it. The most obvious characteristic of the report, the diversity of the opinions expressed therein, turned out, as is suggested above, not to weaken unduly the report's political impact. As a starting point for public debate, that same diversity greatly strengthened it. The argument, both as between the majority report[1] and the Memor-

*The major part of this paper originally appeared as "Kilbrandon: The Ship That Launched a Thousand Faces?" 37 M.L.R. (1974) 544. The author is grateful to the Editors of the Modern Law Review for permission to reproduce it here.

†Professor of Public Law in the University of Dundee.

23

andum of Dissent,[2] and within that majority, was open, thorough and illuminating, clarifying problems and issues in a way no united recommendations could ever have done. Given the nature of the task of the Commission, the absence of such argument would indeed have been strange. The remit was extraordinarily vague; the signatories of the majority report came close to saying so explicitly. Omitting the references to the Channel Islands and the Isle of Man, whose problems are too specialised to concern us here, it was

> "to examine the present functions of the central legislature and government in relation to the several countries, nations, and regions of the United Kingdom; [and] to consider, having regard to developments in local government organisation and in the administrative and other relationships between the various parts of the United Kingdom, and to the interests of the prosperity and good government of our people under the Crown, whether any changes are desirable in those functions or otherwise in present constitutional and economic relationships."

This was certainly far from being clear, unambiguous English: between whom or what, for example, did the constitutional and economic relationships last spoken of subsist? Possibly the nationalistic stirrings which led to the appointment of the Commission commanded the translation of the original terms of reference into Welsh and Gaelic and their re-translation into English, and this was the result. In any event, the Commissioners, not surprisingly, found it impossible even to agree on the kind of inquiry to be conducted, with the majority concentrating their work of detailed examination and their practical recommendations on issues primarily geographical in character, while the authors of the Memorandum of Dissent thought they should look at the system of government as a whole and consider whether it satisfied the needs and aspirations of people in all parts of the United Kingdom.[3]

As a result of this all-embracing approach to constitutional review, the dissentients offered a number of reforms not directly related to the devolutionary issues on which the majority concentrated, such as the creation of a substantial Prime Minister's Department, grouping the Central Policy Review Staff, the Civil Service Department, the Cabinet Office and part of the Treasury; a system of functional Parliamentary committees which would associate Members of Parliament with departmental work of policy formulation; legal regulation of the process of selecting candidates for Parliamentary and other elections, of party expenditure on publicity outside election campaigns and of election broadcasting; and contributions to party expenses from public funds.[4] They were able, moreover, to take account of the long-term constitutional impact of United Kingdom membership of the European Communities in a systematic and comprehensive way, rather than viewing it, as the majority did, purely negatively, as a possible impediment to devolution.[5] They were also bolder than the majority in recommending changes in established institutions flowing naturally from the scheme of devolution they proposed, such as reform of the House of Lords to provide it with a regional element which would interlock Parliament with the new regional organs of government.[6] The majority, guided here perhaps by its interpretation of its terms of reference, rejected this possibility as "unrealistic"[7] and "raising questions extraneous to the question of regional government."[8] Lastly, the freedom offered by a separate Memorandum of Dissent enabled them to present a continuous line of argument leading up to a single specific set of recommendations.

In contrast, the majority, no doubt mindful of the differences among them as to the best concrete solutions, adopted a format in which chapters of general analysis and evaluation of the various possibilities offered — separatism, federalism, the public finance of and general scope for devolution, and its various forms, legislative, executive and administrative, and other variants — were followed by separate chapters putting forward the Commission's several concrete proposals, identifying their respective supporters, and arguing the case for and against them. In this way the general analysis could be presented as unanimous, but inconsistencies do still occur between such views as were presented in these chapters and the views of particular members of the Commission in relation to specific proposals.[9]

The important additional proposals in the Memorandum, the public recrimination over approach and methodology between its authors and those of the Report[10] and the contrast between the exuberant argumentation of the Memorandum and the dispassionate, balanced and sometimes boring analysis of the Report should not be allowed to conceal the fact that the truly fundamental disagreements thrown up by the Commission's inquiry were between a majority group of eight Commissioners[11] who emphasised national identities and favoured legislative devolution with

25

different provisions for Scotland and Wales on the one hand and England on the other, and the minority group of four, two signatories of the Report[12] and the two dissenters, who emphasised equality of political rights and favoured a scheme of executive devolution uniform for the whole of Great Britain.[13] Before looking at these two choices presented by the Commission in more detail, it may be well to mention that the Commission unanimously rejected both the extreme solutions of separatism (because "the vast majority of people simply do not want it to happen"[14]), and federalism ("a strange and artificial system"[15] "alien to our best traditions"[16]), and "minimum change" remedies of increased administrative devolution[17] or a new regional organisation within Parliament.[18]

All the Commissioners agreed that complaints about over-centralisation of government and lack of opportunity for public participation in government were real and warranted the introduction of new representative institutions at regional level (i.e. for Scotland and Wales as a whole and for either eight (Report) or five (Memorandum) English regions). Issue was joined as to what the composition and functions of these institutions should be. The majority felt that the only practicable way in which power could genuinely be transferred from the centre to the regions was by way of legislative devolution, that is, devolution to a regional body of the power, over a defined area of subject-matter, to formulate policies, legislate for their implementation, and carry them into effect. They seemed to feel that only in Scotland and Wales, with their remoteness from London and their well-developed sense of national identity and experience of administrative devolution, was this radical solution necessary and appropriate for the relief of centralisation and the strengthening of democracy. Its extension to the English regions, they thought, was not desired, was not compatible with necessary central powers of economic co-ordination and general policy-making and was apparently not necessary for the remedying of English discontent about government.[19] They therefore proposed the institution of different kinds of regional body for Scotland and Wales on the one hand and the English regions on the other.

For Scotland and Wales, it was suggested,[20] there should be established single-chamber assemblies of about 100 members directly elected for a fixed term of four years by the single transferable vote system of proportional representation, with power to legislate in their area on a wide range of subjects (largely co-extensive with the present range of responsibilities of the Scottish and Welsh Offices). Hence they would be competent in matters such as health, education, housing, agriculture and town and country planning, and the Scottish assembly would, largely because of the needs of a separate Scottish legal system, have additional responsibilities in such fields as police, law reform and administration of justice.[21] Parliament would, however, retain over-riding legislative authority, much as under section 75 of the Government of Ireland Act 1920 (or section 4 (4) of the Northern Ireland Constitution Act 1973) and there would be a further safeguard in that the central government, with the approval of Parliament, would have a reserve power to prevent any assembly measure going for the Royal Assent (e.g. a measure inconsistent with international obligations of the United Kingdom). Executive functions would be discharged by ministers drawn from among the members of the assembly and operating according to the conventions of cabinet government, rather than through the local authority system of administration by committees of the assembly. The finance of the two regional governments thus constituted would be largely supplied by way of grant from the United Kingdom government, but might also be alimented by a share of the United Kingdom taxes and by certain devolved taxes such as petrol duty, vehicle excise duty or a retail sales tax.[22] Each regional government would be entitled as a minimum to an annual grant equal to the cost of maintaining in the region United Kingdom standards of provision of the devolved services, less the region's share of shared taxes and the sum which the devolved taxes would produce for the region if levied at the rates applying in the rest of the United Kingdom. The ascertainment and costing of United Kingdom standards of provision would be a quinquennial task for a new body, an independent statutory regional exchequer board,[23] which would also determine each year, on the basis of the regional government's own budget and the representations of the Treasury, the amount of grant the region should actually receive. Scotland and Wales would continue to send a substantial, but somewhat reduced, number of members to Parliament, and would continue to be represented in the United Kingdom Cabinet, not by Secretaries of State, but by ministers with other responsibilities as well.

For England, on the other hand, the only proposal the majority had to make[24] was for a system of regional councils, largely indirectly elected by local authorities, but with a minority (one fifth) of members appointed by the central government, with the function of publicly discussing, and advising and making representations on, the activities and plans of central government, local government and *ad hoc* bodies, such as nationalised industries or water and hospital authorities, in and for their respective regions. Essentially, this is a proposal to strengthen somewhat the existing regional economic planning councils, which presents, by reason of its very limited extent, a startling contrast with the full-blooded legislative devolution recommended for Scotland and Wales. Since, by the majority's own admission, such councils "could do little to correct the centralising tendencies of government"[25] and since they do not offer substantially increased opportunities for participation in, or democratic control of, government decisions, the ultimate position of the majority could be harshly, but perhaps not inaccurately, represented as one of offering no solution to discontents with government operating in England, while offering to Scotland and Wales, for the relief of those same discontents, a solution which apparently would not work under English conditions. Quite clearly, therefore, the "national feeling" of the Scots and Welsh was for the majority the magic ingredient which would turn devolution from a dangerous drug into a panacea for all constitutional ills.

The choice by the minority of equality of political rights as their starting point led them, as might have been expected, into a very different devolutionary adventure.[26] The majority proposals for legislative devolution to Scotland and Wales alone were offensive to this principle, involving as they did a double representation for the Scots and Welsh — in the regional assembly and the Westminster Parliament — but not for the English, and the possibility of Scottish and Welsh M.P.s participating in decisions at Westminster on "domestic" English issues.[27] Their view of what was practicable was also radically different from that of the majority. For them, to confer on Scottish and Welsh assemblies, let alone English ones, a *de facto* exclusive power to legislate in limited areas ran contrary to an irresistible trend of harmonisation of policy at supranational levels, particularly in the context of the European Communities. The ability to adopt independent policies would be but a paper one, and growing awareness of this would produce dangerous frustrations. *A contrario*, an executive devolution, leaving all broad issues of policy formulation in the hands of the United Kingdom government and Parliament (or of the institutions of the European Communites, but giving regional assemblies and governments a large role and measure of discretion in their implementation, would alleviate over the whole of the United Kingdom the present discontents with over-centralisation and lack of participation, would respect the principle of equality and would be quite workable.

Though presented differently, the schemes in the Report and the Memorandum were remarkably similar in substance. Each involved the creation in Scotland and Wales and each of eight (or five) English regions of an assembly, again of 100 members elected for a fixed four-year term by single transferable vote, and of a regional executive operating within that assembly through the kind of committee system familiar in local authorities. Each regional government (as assembly and executive together may conveniently be styled) would take over the administrative (as opposed to the policy-forming) functions of central government in its area over a wide range of matters, wider than that envisaged for legislative devolution,[28] but with the same core of existing Scottish and Welsh Office functions. This would involve the transfer of most regional organisations of central government departments to the new regional governments, together with certain responsibilities for supervising local authorities and supervising (or actually carrying out the work of) *ad hoc* authorities such as water and regional health authorities. The signatories of the Memorandum of Dissent (but not, apparently, the other two members of the minority) also envisaged that the assemblies might have a general power to make ordinances for the benefit of their areas, a big brother to the present by-law making power of local authorities, exercised subject to central government veto. Liaison with central government would be assured by the continuance of ministerial representation in Cabinet on a reduced scale, either through a single minister responsible for liaison with all regional governments, or through three such ministers, one each for Scotland, Wales and England; and with Parliament, by means either of a special statutory council of regional representatives which would require to be consulted about proposals for Parliamentary legislation affecting regions, or via reform of the House of Lords to include a regional element. Scottish and Welsh representation in the House of Commons would be undiminished.

The main difference between the Report and the Memorandum was on the question of finance. The two signatories of the Report envisaged that all finance for the region would eventually be provided by block grant from the Treasury, whose size would be determined by government and Parliament without the intervention of an Exchequer Board, and which would not be supplemented by any kind of shared or devolved taxation.[29] The Memorandum, on the other hand, presented two different financial schemes,[30] both of which, for reasons of regional independence and financial responsibility, relied on the raising of a substantial amount of money from regional taxes. These two schemes differed, however, on the question of whether the supplementary grant from the central government was to be based solely on need, as determined by objective standards, or on a mixture of need and financial capacity, but agreed with each other and with the "minority of the majority" in rejecting the institution of any independent arbitral body to make such determinations.

The slipperiness of the distinction between policy and administration will be familiar to all students of constitutional law and public administration, and the principal criticism of this scheme by the majority was that it would entail drawing some such distinction in relation to every one of thousands of governmental tasks which are arguably suitable for devolution.[31] To make a vertical distinction of this kind work, it is essential first that Parliament should begin to legislate in a manner radically different from its present one — that is, with less attention to administrative detail and more explicit enunciation of general principles — and second, that the relationship between choice of legal instruments and generality of policy be rationalised, so that we do not, as is presently the case in the educational field, make major policy decisions like the switch to comprehensive secondary education by administrative circular, while requiring statutory instruments for matters of administrative detail like school building standards. It was symptomatic of the general attitude of the majority to its task that it should have considered the need for these consequential changes, arguably highly desirable in themselves as conducing to greater openness and democracy in government, as a disadvantage of the scheme.[32] Even if it were possible to rationalise rule-making in this way, the task of deciding what is important enough to be dealt with centrally and what regionally is by no means an easy one. The suggestion of the Memorandum that the regional government should "take over the control of, and responsibility for, virtually all the outposts of central government now operating in their areas"[33] has an attractive but on close examination spurious simplicity; a division of responsibility between central and regional offices of Great Britain departments cannot be automatically valid for the quite different situation of division between bodies responsible to separate central and regional assemblies, possibly of different political complexions; and similarly, the range of responsibilities of the Scottish and Welsh Offices has been determined in the context of the operation of these departments as an integral part of the central government, not as the executive arm of independent assemblies. A task by task division of governmental functions is therefore necessary, and the Memorandum did indeed indicate, in a lengthy appendix, how this might be done in the fields of education and housing.[34]

Scrutiny of the majority and minority proposals from the standpoint of the lawyer — and particularly the lawyer in Scotland — discloses some disquieting features. While the majority proposed to create for Scotland and Wales legislatures whose status, functions, and mode of operation would bear strong similarities to those of the Stormont Parliament established in 1973, and which might, notwithstanding the system of proportional representation recommended for their election, likewise be dominated over long periods by a single party, it saw no need to limit the potential of those assemblies for arbitrary and oppressive action by way of the enactment by Parliament either of a judicially enforceable Bill of Rights to which they would be subject, or of arrangements for the institution of machinery for the redress of grievances such as the regional Ombudsmen recommended by the Memorandum or a developed system of administrative justice such as obtains in West Germany, to whose governmental arrangements the Commission paid considerable attention. "A fully developed system of administrative law" was summarily dismissed as "absent in the United Kingdom and, it might be thought, alien to our tradition"[35]; Ombudsmen figure nowhere in the Report's schemes of devolution; and "the requirement in Northern Ireland for provisions against discrimination" (recognised in sections 17-23 of the Northern Ireland Constitution Act 1973) "arises out of the existence of a community problem which is peculiar to the Province; ... there would be no need to include in the Westminster legislation establishing the assemblies statutory provisions designed to ensure the preservation of basic human rights of a kind which in some overseas countries are enshrined in Bills of Rights."[36]

This is a bold statement, and if we look back to the main argu-

31

ment on the matter in paragraphs 749-755 of the Report, we find that it rests on two very slender supports. The first is the argument that the region would not be a sovereign state: Parliament would retain ultimate power in all matters, and could therefore intervene in the last resort if the assemblies were to infringe or fail to protect essential human rights. This is open to three substantial objections: first, it will doubtless be difficult, and rightly so, to discuss at Westminster and to question United Kingdom government ministers about matters falling within the competence of assemblies for which they have no responsibility[37]; second, legislation, which is the only method of intervention left to Parliament in the scheme of legislative devolution, is an ineffective and inappropriate way of righting the individual wrongs which *ex hypothesi* will have occurred when Parliament is moved to act; third, the generally low sensitivity of Parliament to human rights issues, the tendency for arguments of principle to be swept aside in favour of administrative convenience or party politics,[38] and the history of Westminster's relations with Stormont together suggest that Parliamentary intervention in regional affairs is unlikely even when important derogations from human rights occur.[39]

Secondly, it was argued that if a Bill of Rights was necessary for the regions, then it must be no less necessary at the centre. This latter innovation was out of the question for the Commission as "it does not arise specificaly out of the devolutionary proposals we have examined" and "because there is no evidence that the public conscience ... is not adequate to provide the protection called for."[40] In consequence, the former innovation was apparently out of the question also. To this argument there are likewise three objections. First, many (the writer among them) would dispute the adequacy of the public conscience in these matters; second, if the majority is going to argue from central to regional government in this way, then the question of a United Kingdom Bill of Rights does most definitely arise out of devolutionary proposals; and third, it is a complete *non sequitur* to argue from central government, where the even balance of political forces constantly drives both parties to seek consensus and the middle ground, to regional government which (to cite one distinguished contributor to this volume quoting another) "creates the possibility that there will make itself heard in government the voice of a local opinion so extreme [that] ...it creates the need for protective institutions hitherto disdained by the traditions and conventions of Parliamentary democracy at Westminster."[41] It is far from certain that the results of proportional representation and the need to operate within an assembly of fixed duration would together be sufficient to create conditions which would reproduce in the regions the naturally centripetal effect of the balance of political forces at Westminster, and hence make it appropriate to judge the need for a Bill of Rights for the regions by the same criteria as for the centre.

The problem of protection of human rights did not arise with the same urgency in relation to the scheme of executive devolution presented by the minority; here, there would be ample opportunities for judicial control, by way of the doctrine of *ultra vires*, of regional implementation of the policies formulated in statutory form at the centre. While, in consequence, it paid no heed to problems of human rights, the Memorandum did adopt the fashionable panacea of the Ombudsman for the remedying of individual grievances, suggesting the appointment of one for each region, directly accessible to members of the public and not limited in his inquiries to questions of maladministration.[42]

The legal problems of the minority scheme arise specifically in relation to Scotland, which has not only a distinct judicial system and a separate criminal and civil law, but also much separate legislation more or less paralleling English legislation, particularly in the fields of administration for which the Scottish Office is presently responsible. Thus the English Housing Acts, Agriculture Acts and Education Acts are all paralleled by Housing (Scotland), Agriculture (Scotland) and Education (Scotland) Acts, a practice which permits both the adaptation of common policies to the distinctive framework of Scottish civil and criminal law, and numerous (and sometimes important) policy variants to suit specifically Scottish conditions and *mores*.[43] It is not clear that either group of members of the minority gave serious thought to the devolutionary problems created by the guaranteed[44] existence of a separate system of Scots law (which for the majority, of course, was one of the reasons for recommending legislative devolution in Scotland).[45] All assumed the transfer of the Scottish Office's administrative functions to the regional government; and given the new style of policy-formulating central legislation on which the whole scheme of executive devolution depends, such responsibilities might well include the drafting of measures for the adaptation of policies to the particular legal framework afforded by Scots law. But the minority signatories of the main

Report envisaged the disappearance of the Secretary of State for Scotland from the United Kingdom government and the consequent transfer of policy-formulating functions for Scotland to the Great Britain departments: for example, the Department of the Environment, in respect of town and country planning in Scotland as in England, the Department of Education and Science in respect of primary and secondary education and so on. As the Report pointed out in its general chapter sketching the pros and cons of executive devolution, "while there would be some logic in this in a scheme of general devolution, it is difficult to believe that the Scots and the Welsh would not regard it as a retrograde step."[46] Certainly, its effect would be to eliminate the specifically Scottish voice in the policy-making process that can be heard under the present system, and to leave without appropriate ministerial support or means of legislative development the distinct Scottish civil and criminal law. Who, for example, would appoint the Scottish Law Commission or the members of the Court of Session? Who would pilot through Parliament legislation to reform, say, the law of succession in Scotland?

The dissentients seemed to see this problem rather more clearly but provided no straightforward answer to it. They recommended the continuation of some specifically Scottish (and Welsh) representation in the United Kingdom Cabinet, albeit on a non-departmental basis.[47] This would permit ministerial representatives of Scottish and Welsh interests to influence policy-making for the United Kingdom as a whole, without actually playing a central part in it, which is possibly not very different from the present position. They explicitly recognised the existence of Scottish criminal law,[48] and perhaps made a bow in the direction of civil law when suggesting that the Scottish assembly and government would have a wider range of administrative (*sic*) functions than those of the English regions because of "the special nature of Scottish law" generally.[49] It seemed to be envisaged that the Scottish regional government would be able to use its powers to make ordinances for the good government and general welfare of the people of its area, outside the framework of specific United Kingdom policies and subject to central government consent, to reform, as necessary, the Scottish system of criminal law, and possibly the civil law system as well.[50] If this were not to be the case, then again, Scots law would be left without appropriate governmental oversight or avenues of development, in that it would possibly become a minor responsibility of some Great Britain department, a totally unacceptable solution. On the other hand, if the Scottish government did receive this competence, then important elements of legislative devolution would enter into the minority scheme as it affects Scotland and there would be a substantial weakening of the principle of equality of political rights to which the authors attached such weight. Scottish M.P.s at Westminster would be able to participate in (or perhaps block) reform of the English divorce laws, but reform of the Scottish divorce laws would be a matter for the Scottish assembly alone, subject to a central government veto, the grounds for whose exercise are hard to imagine. Whatever their other merits, in short, schemes of purely executive devolution do not chime well with the existence of two separate systems of law within Great Britain, and for Scotland at least, a combined scheme of legislative and executive devolution, along lines explained in the majority Report,[51] seems likely to be the upshot even of the minority proposals.

A third point, which runs through both Reports, is of more general concern. Its essence is expressed elsewhere in this volume in David Williams' comment, "it is remarkable that such an interaction of law and convention should be contemplated in advance for an entirely new system of government."[52] It may be that one of the weaknesses of lawyers as political animals is their desire to state positions clearly, to see things cut and dried, when much of the art of politics consists in surrounding one's standpoints with areas of indefiniteness into which one can move if pressure on the position becomes too great. At the same time, undue respect for this wisdom by those entrusted with reformative tasks carries the risk that the need for the fundamental decisions essential to the reform proposed will be disguised or evaded; that the constitutional *status quo ante* will be quietly preserved amid the flourishes of change; and that the resultant frustration and dissatisfaction of the supposed beneficiaries of reform will be worse than ever before. The whole Kilbrandon Commission has arguably fallen into this trap, by refusing to contemplate, at many points, the adequate legal safeguards which will furnish an expression of the intended shift of power sufficiently unambivalent to make it impossible to resist or reverse *sub silentio*.

Excellent examples of this indeterminateness are furnished by the proposals of the Report and Memorandum in the vital field of finance. Thus the majority sought to make the determination of the amount and basis of the government's block grant to the regions a matter for independent "adjudication" by the Exchequer Board, after receiving "representations" from the Treasury. Necessary though this might be to provide the regional governments with a sentiment of genuine freedom and independence, the majority shrank from the proposal's implications of restriction of governmental and Parliamentary power: the upshot of this independent adjudication was not to be decisions by the Board, but "recommendations" to the central government, presented "in the firm expectation that they would be accepted."[53] The legislative designation of the status of the Board's conclusions would, of course, in no way express the sentiment of this rider, and would provide an imperturbable cover beneath which the recommendations of the Board might either be reduced to formal expressions of what the Treasury had decided anyway or be amended every year, at an ever decreasing cost in political embarrassment. The schemes of the Memorandum demonstrate a similar fudging of the different question of whether one can reconcile a worthwhile degree of financial independence for the regions with the retention of a genuine and effective policy-making power in the hands of central government. Final responsibility for determining the size of regional expenditure was left clearly to the central government, but there was equivocation over its powers in regard to the composition of regional governments' expenditure programmes. Central government approval of the programme was to be based, *inter alia*, on the consistency of the regional government's expenditure pattern with "the responsibilities placed on it by central government;"[54] yet at the same time "the central government would not normally be expected to seek to alter the pattern of functional expenditure proposed by a [regional] government."[55] Again, such expectations cannot be legislated for, and once the possibility — be it never so rare — of detailed alteration is accepted, the legal power must be formulated so as to provide for it, and may therefore, as with the Exchequer Board above, provide cover for a continuing diminution of the freedom that the reforms were designed to achieve. Experience should have taught that in financial matters, conventions like these are far too frail a support for changes in the location of decision-making power. The treatment of the Parliamentary Boundary Commissioners' recommendations in 1969,[56] and the continuing increase of government control over the details of some nationalised industries' investment programmes,[57] illustrate this truth in a way that is highly apposite to these Kilbrandon proposals.

These legal problems thrown up by the Report and the Memorandum of Dissent exemplify the defects of the one and the other document. On the one hand, there is the "tunnel vision" of the signatories of the Report, straining so hard (yet unsuccessfully) to focus on a single devolutionary proposal that they dared not look around to see the constitutional problems they were passing by; on the other, the obsession of the dissentients with comprehensiveness and uniformity, which led them to neglect the implications for their scheme of reform even of existing institutionalised differences between the various parts of the United Kingdom. On both hands there is apparently an unlawyerlike belief that one can successfully initiate major constitutional changes by enacting laws which are not supposed to mean what they say. If, however, neither document carries within itself the solution to our constitutional ills, together they make a massive and invaluable contribution to informing a debate about devolution which seems likely to continue for as long as North Sea oil provides fuel to feed the nationalists' tongues of flame.

NOTES

1. Royal Commission on the Constitution 1969-1973, Vol. I, Report, Cmnd. 5460 (1973); hereinafter referred to as "Report".
2. Royal Commission on the Constitution 1969-1973, Vol . II, Memorandum of Dissent by Lord Crowther-Hunt and Professor A.T. Peacock, Cmnd. 5460-I (1973); hereinafter referred to as "Memorandum".
3. It is unfortunate that while arguing that the majority construed the Commission's terms of reference too narrowly, the authors of the Memorandum should themselves be unable to state them correctly: Memorandum, paras. 1-4.
4. Memorandum, paras. 280-296, 311-316.
5. Compare Memorandum, paras. 83-113, with Report, paras. 403-415.
6. Memorandum, paras. 297-307.
7. Report, para. 858.
8. Report, para. 1073.
9. Compare paras. 670-678 with para. 1163, or para. 910 with para. 1169.
10. Report, paras. 14, 29-32; Memorandum, Preface, and para. 119.
11. Lord Kilbrandon, Mr. Alun Davies, Sir Mark Henig, Dr. Longmuir, Professors Newark and Street, Sir Ben Bowen Thomas, and Mrs. Trenaman. This majority includes all the non-English members of the Commission.

12. Lord Foot and Sir James Steel.

13. The thirteenth and last Commissioner, Sir David Renton, cannot be bracketed with either of these groups; his scheme is *sui generis* (at least in relation to Scotland), involving neither legislative nor executive devolution: Report, paras. 1174-1187.

14. Report, para. 497.

15. Report, para. 539.

16. Memorandum, para. 116.

17. Report, chap. 21.

18. Report, chap. 22.

19. Report, paras. 1188, 1208.

20. See generally Report, paras. 1125-1153.

21. For the full list of functions, see Report, para. 1132. Two members of the majority group (Professor Street and Mrs. Trenaman) were of the view that because of the absence of a separate Welsh system of law or a substantial body of distinct Welsh legislation, a Welsh assembly should be restricted to advisory and consultative functions: Report, paras. 1174-1183.

22. On the scope for devolving taxes, see Report, para 624 and Appendix C.

23. The composition and functions of such a board are discussed in detail in Report, paras. 670-678.

24. See generally, Report, paras. 1195-1209.

25. Report, para. 965.

26. See generally Report, paras. 1154-1173, Memorandum, paras. 208-279.

27. Memorandum, paras. 126-129.

28. Certain administrative functions in relation to trade and industry, for example, might also be taken over.

29. Report, paras. 1163.

30. Memorandum, paras. 262-276 and Appendix B.

31. Report, para. 1171.

32. Report, para. 1193.

33. Memorandum, para. 211(a).

34. Memorandum, Appendix C.

35. Report, para. 850.

36. Report, para. 1328.

37. The Report, it is true, envisaged Parliamentary participation in the process of giving Royal Assent to assembly legislation (para. 764-767), but concrete questions of disregard of human rights are much more likely to arise in the implementation of such legislation than on the face of the legislation itself.

38. Consider, for example, recent retrospective legislation passed to deprive private parties of the fruits of litigation asserting basic human rights: War Damage Act 1964, reversing Burmah Oil (Burma Trading) Co. Ltd. v. Lord Advocate, 1964 S.C. (H.L.) 117, [1965] A.C. 75 (compensation for war damage); Education (Scotland) Act 1973, reversing Malloch v. Aberdeen Corporation (No. 2) [1973] 1 All E.R. 304 (H.L.) (natural justice).

39. E.g. the effective disenfranchisement of many anti-Unionist voters in

Northern Ireland through the abolition of proportional representation, and substitution of the relative majority system, by the House of Commons (Method of Voting and Redistribution of Seats) Act (N.I.) 1929.

40. Report, para. 755.
41. Bradley, "Some Constitutional Aspects of Scottish Development," in Wolfe, ed., Government and Nationalism in Scotland, 41-50, 46 (1969), quoting Calvert, Constitutional Law in Northern Ireland, 5 (1968).
42. Memorandum, para. 261.
43. A small but cogent example of such adaptations is provided by the fact that the Shops Act 1950, re-enacting earlier English and Scottish statutes, prohibits virtually all Sunday opening of shops in England and Wales, but, in its application to Scotland, prohibits only the Sunday opening of barbers' shops. The reason for this peculiar differentiation is that while in Scotland, unlike England, "social pressures and the fear of the Kirk courts combined to ensure that the Sabbath was not broken by a significant number of people," the intervention of the law had at one point been thought necessary "to counter a specific evil, namely the practice of resorting to shaving shops in preference to attending Church service." Quotations are from Dawson, "The Fourth Commandment" 1974 S.L.T. (News) 129, a succinct account of the peculiar law of the Scottish Sunday which furnishes, in microcosm, much food for thought regarding the need for, and the difficulties of, the various devolutionary proposals under discussion.
44. By Articles XVIII and XIX of the Treaty of Union 1707.
45. Report, para. 1150.
46. Report, para. 910.
47. Memorandum, para. 289.
48. Memorandum, para. 220.
49. Memorandum, note to para. 223.
50. Memorandum, paras. 220-222.
51. Report, paras. 912-914.
52. Infra, p. 72.
53. Report, para. 673. Para. 676, however, talks of "decisions" which could be overturned by the House of Commons on the advice of the government.
54. Memorandum, para. 274(c).
55. Memorandum, para. 275.
56. See de Smith, Constitutional and Administrative Law 247-248 (2nd ed., 1973), for the story.
57. It is instructive to contrast the emphasis, in Ministerial statements explaining the statutory provisions for control over investment, on the broad and global character of the control, with the item-by-item scrutiny involved in some modern investment reviews: see, e.g. House of Commons Standing Committee Debates 1947-48, vol. IV, col. 653 (explaining s. 5(2), Electricity Act 1947); Select Committee on Nationalised Industries, Ministerial Control of the Nationalised Industries (1967-68) H.C. 371-III, Appendix 34 (Memorandum by British Railways Board on relations between the Ministry of Transport and the British Railways Board on capital investment matters).

IV WHO WANTS DEVOLUTION?

Kilbrandon — a different view of the evidence

Harry Calvert*

As contributors to this volume and most other commentators have noted the members of the Kilbrandon Commission differed considerably amongst themselves as to the structure of government which they thought apt for the United Kingdom at this point in its history. An even more obvious point deserves rather more attention than it has received. The members of the Commission are unanimous on the need for some extension of the present scope of intermediate level vertical devolution.

This is a view with which I happen to agree, but I do not feel entirely happy with the reasoning which leads the Commission to this view. Since the reasons for devolving are likely to colour the type of devolution one opts for, it is not merely academic to question the reasons. I hope I do not perpetrate too great an injustice to members of the Commission if I classify their reasons in the following manner:

1. Some form of devolution is a rational response to certain established and agreed deficiencies in our present system of government.
2. Expert evidence is in favour of an extension of the present scope of vertical devolution.
3. There is a sufficient popular demand for devolution for it to be necessary.

I agree with the first of these reasons and will advert later and briefly to the defects which devolution might be harnessed to remove. In this paper I wish to question the second and third reasons, devoting, however, greater effort to assaulting the third.[1] First, however, a few comments about the second.

* Professor of Law, University of Newcastle-upon-Tyne.

The Experts

I use the term "experts" in a broad sense, including elected and appointed personnel in central and local government, members of regional bodies, students of government, etc. The first comment I wish to make about such evidence is that by reason of the way in which Royal Commissions go about their business, the range of such witnesses may tend to be biassed in the direction of self-selection. I do not wish to make much of this; merely to say that it perhaps ought not to surprise us if the evidence in favour of an extension of devolution seems to be rather more aggressive and vociferated than that in favour of maintaining the status quo. The advocates of change do tend to be more vociferous and are perhaps more likely to seize an opportunity to express their views when the occasion offers itself, especially if there seems to be a prospect of something actually being done.

The second comment I wish to make on this evidence is this. As one reads the evidence, and the comments of the Commission on it, one realises that whilst the general tenor of evidence from within central government is *against*, that from regional and local government is overwhelmingly *for* an extension of vertical devolution. The Commission seems to be influenced rather more by the latter, impressionistically sketching the personality of the typical witness and seeming to accept the reliability of his judgment as to what is wrong and what is needed to put it right (Report, paras. 271-272). The dissenters draw similar conclusions (Memorandum, paras. 33-35). On some matters, such as that people in local and regional government *feel* dissatisfied, I am happy to accept the evidence. On other matters, especially as to what needs to be done, I am rather reluctant to accept the evidence which is to the effect that the power and influence of the witness should be increased and extended. And the interest of the witness is not the only reason for scepticism. As the Commission itself points out (though here as elsewhere, having made the point it seems thereafter to ignore it) the evidence is sometimes necessarily based on partial ignorance; and it also tends to conflict with the evidence of more detached witnesses, such as students of government, which tends to focus upon devices for abating popular dissatisfaction, rather than having any special affection for devolution as such.

I wish, however, to concern myself mainly with the evidence consisting of an alleged popular demand for devolution.

Public opinion

Public opinion is relevant to the work of the Commission in at least two ways which are never clearly distinguished by the Commission. It is first of all the best evidence, indeed, it is the fact, of any feelings of dissatisfaction which there might be in the people at large with our existing system of government. Secondly, if one subscribes to some democratic principle such as that the people should have the form of government they want, then what they want will obviously be an important determinant in what is done. It is important to note, however, that the people might, irrationally, want something which is not particularly relevant to removing the sources of their dissatisfaction with the existing system. Thus, if one dare be rather less than wholeheartedly democratic, one might accept the evidence as to dissatisfaction but prefer a more rational approach to its removal. In fact, I do not believe that public opinion as to what form of government we should have is irrational in relation to public discontent. In this, I disagree with both the majority and the minority of the Commission. The disagreement centres around the significance to be attached to the findings of the Attitudes Survey (Research Paper No. 7).

The Attitudes Survey

The Commission decided at an early stage that it should do what it could to find out the views of the general public and the Government Social Survey was accordingly briefed in the terms set out in Appendix A hereto. I shall come to the particular survey we are here concerned with in a moment, but first a few reminders about attitudes surveys in general:
1. Attitudes may be ephemeral and/or volatile. The investigators themselves were aware that limitations were imposed upon them, in enquiring about attitudes towards certain functions of government, by the fact that opinion might have been artificially distorted by the general election of 1970; and the authors of the Memorandum of Dissent rightly point out that the value of the Survey might have increased had the investigations been spread or repeated. The Commission did, after all, deliberate for 4½ years.
2. As is well-known and obvious, but nevertheless worthy of repetition, the information elicited by interview and questionnaire is information merely about what the interviewee

43

says his attitude is. His attitude may, of course, actually *be* what he *says*, but there are many reasons why it might not. Interview is an artificial social situation and the interviewee may well be affected by his conception of the social relationship which confronts him. The interviewer may be of a different age, sex, social class or educational attainment, all of which factors may affect the answers. Thus, the interviewee may assert that he has an attitude when in fact he doesn't in an attempt to supply what he thinks is expected of him, or as a consequence of the role which the situation seems to thrust upon him. There is also a marked tendency to gravitate towards the moderate opinion, expressing itself in a disposition to agree mildly with a proposition put or to prefer the middle of three alternatives offered. This fact obviously makes it possible, even unconsciously, to load the results by framing the proposition in a particular way, or by selecting an unrepresentative range of options. This happens in the Attitudes Survey and I shall illustrate it later. Some of the above limitations are, however, well illustrated by one part of the Survey to which I shall not return. Table 27 reveals that, asked to agree strongly or a little, or disagree strongly or a little, 78% of informants agreed that "Most people who work in large organisations would like more say in the way their job is done", whilst 69% agree with a proposition later put, that "Most people who work in large organisations are quite happy to get on with their jobs and to leave management problems to the managers" (and 68% thought that "Most employers and managers don't give people who work for them enough say in how things are run".) It is possible, by cunning parsing and resort to secondary meanings, to effect a sort of reconciliation of these statements, but not so as to convince me that at least a half of the interviewees appeared both to believe that most people who work in large organisations would like more say in the way their job is done *and* are quite happy to get on with their jobs and leave management problems to the managers. At best one is left in perplexity as to the attitudes thus evidenced.

3. A further vice of research by interview and questionnaire is that in the very nature of the method, the interviewee is inevitably led. With a questionnaire, the extent will be obvious, but with oral interview (or "probing" in connection with a questionnaire) we cannot know the extent as readily. If one

takes the subject of public opinion in relation to hooliganism, it must be obvious how leading would be such a question as "Do you favour the issuing of passes to juveniles as a means of combatting hooliganism?" addressed to an interviewee who had never had a prior thought on the subject. If one tries to minimise the "leading" one ends up with some question such as "Is anything worrying you?" and follows it by an interminable series of coaxing questions equally unconfining. Even "Is anything worrying you?" is leading. It is not practically possible to avoid this vice entirely, but it is possible to minimise it and I shall suggest later that the Attitudes Survey fails in this respect.

4. Notoriously, results have to be interpreted, and we all know how statistical information can be abused. An additional point worth mentioning is that whilst we are on our guard against misinterpretation by users of the Survey report, we are less vigilant about misinterpretation by the reporters themselves. We tend to assume that they simply observe and report matters of fact. This is not so. The Attitudes Survey, as will be seen later, regularly interprets the facts in its tabulation of them, and, as the authors of the Memorandum point out, engages in further interpretation in its commentary on the results, "seriously underplay(ing) its own evidence" according to the dissenters (para. 39). This is in fact important since the Report frequently draws upon this commentary, rather than the raw results, in making out its case for devolution.

Many of these vices are evidenced in the work to which the Survey is put by the Commission. Here are some examples:

(a) Asked whether they thought that government understood the needs of their region better than those of other regions, 31% in London answered "yes" by comparison with 10% in the country as a whole. The Report (para. 292) regards this as "showing that in people's minds at least geographical proximity to government may be an advantage". It does not. It merely shows that there are more people of the opinion asked above in London than average and gives no reason whatever for attributing these opinions to geographical factors.

(b) The Survey revealed that a substantial minority of people (perhaps 20 to 25%) considered that they had the basic ability to play some part in government. The Report (para.

45

314) concludes that "the potential is there". This, of course, confuses the fact that they are able (which is not at all established) with the fact that they *think* they are able (which is established). The potential may not be there at all; or it may be much greater than is assumed.

(c) At paragraph 369, the Report states that ". . . the answers given in Scotland and Wales (re satisfaction with the understanding by government of the needs of regions) reflected an above average level of discontent." This is literally true; but it is equally as true of other regions, such as the South-West and the North which are virtually indistinguishable from Wales in this regard. One is thus "guided" towards the view that special treatment for Scotland and Wales is justified.

(d) There is a similar, barely susceptible nudge, in paragraph 371 where, after noting that 20% of people in Scotland and 9% of people in Wales had spontaneously suggested "home rule" etc., as an improvement they would like to see, the Commission conclude that "the findings are significant in assessing attitudes to devolution." The significance is not specified; but if it is the obvious, i.e. that in spite of the frequent public discussion of the concept in these two areas, 80% of Scots and 91% of Welshmen do not even mention it when offered the opportunity of volunteering suggestions for improvement, it seems strangely disregarded by the Commission in making recommendations.

These are some of the causes of my scepticism. Others will be mentioned later. I come now to the particular survey with which we are here concerned and the uses to which it is put.

Attitudes towards Devolution

The Commission had, in its brief to the Government Social Survey, expressly asked for answers to certain questions affecting possible forms of devolution (Appendix A). In its questionnaires, the Survey proceeded from asking questions about general attitudes toaards government calculated to focus upon dissatisfaction and discontent, to asking questions concerning devolution and, inevitably, presenting devolution to some extent as a possible remedy for the dissatisfaction. The questionnaires, indeed, seem almost designed (though I do not suggest at all that they actually were

46

designed) to evoke responses favourable to devolution from subjects. The first 16 questions probe for grievances. The questionnaires then, without notice, proceed to crystallise regional
associations in the interviewee (questions 17-21), leading to the
question: ". . . what would you like to see done to improve things
in (your region)" (question 22), something of a have-you-
stopped-beating-your-wife question, especially in view of the
fact that the interviewee is immediately prompted to judgement
on specific services in his region (question 23) and comparisons
with other parts of Britain (questions 24 and 25). Question 26
then blandly assumes that the subject will have some degree of
enthusiasm for various forms of associating government with
regions, including making sure that M.P.s have stronger
regional ties, government taking more trouble to understand the
region's *special* needs (italics supplied), having more decisions
made in the region, making it easier for people in the regions to
explain their special problems to the government and allowing
an M.P. to have more influence over what the government does in
the region. Only the most rigorous and brave-hearted sheep
would, at that point, have resisted the shepherding. And few who
allowed themselves to speculate that regional devices *might* have
some relevance would later opt for "leaving things as they are at
present" (questions 27 and 28) or characterise an extension of
regional government as being "simply a change for the sake of
change making no real difference" (question 29). This has further implications:

In another way, the form of the questionnaires built in a bias
towards an extension of regional government. The alternatives
presented to interviewees in answering many questions are exem-
plified by question 28(a) to which I shall return. In this question,
"For running the region as a whole" (itself begging the question
whether one should think in terms of "regions" at all for purposes of "running things"), the interviewee is offered five
choices: "(1) leaving things as they are; (2) keeping things much
as they are but making sure government understands regional
needs better; (3) keeping the present system but allowing more
decisions to be made in the region; (4) having a new system of governing the region so that as many decisions as possible are made
in the area (*sic*, i.e. not "the region"); and (5) letting the region
take over complete responsibility for running things in the
region." We already have some devolution. Why, then, not offer
the interviewee the choice of (1) much less; (2) less; (3) the same;

(4) more; (5) much more devolution than at present? The range of options actually offered makes it highly probable that the scatter of responses will concentrate in the area of extension of devolution.

The Commission, in its Report, rightly adverts to the question mark which such procedures must inevitably put against the answers, though in attributing the entire blame to the limitations which it imposed in its brief the Commission is being too harsh on itself and too soft on the investigators. The responses would have inspired greater confidence had the questions on devolution preceded those probing for discontent, and had their "leading" character been minimised. As it is, and as the Commission states (para. 268): "It must be recognised . . . that if a person is dissatisfied, and he is presented with only one suggested remedy, then he may be expected to take a generally favourable view of this remedy, whatever it is, even if he has given no previous thought to it." One could only wish that the Commission had taken this *caveat* more to heart for there is little evidence, in the pages that follow, that the Commission in fact did seriously question the validity of the results obtained.

The limitations imposed by the brief and the form of the questionnaires and method of inquiry, then, must cause any prudent man to have the gravest doubts about the evidence thus obtained. It might have been better to forget the Survey as a brave but failed attempt; and it is perfectly true that the Commission uses the Survey results really only as supplementary evidence. It is, however, as I have suggested, rather weak evidence which is thus supplemented. This is the main burden of this paper. The discussion of the Survey results which follows, and the comments on the use to which they were put, is all subject to this fundamental vice.

The Survey Results.

The Survey results, not surprisingly, do seem to reveal attitudes of interest, of various degrees, in regional government, of various types. Thus, the answers to question 28(a), described above, are shown in Appendix B. It is interesting, here, to contrast two ways of commenting on these results. The Survey Report itself states (p.63):

"A quarter wanted no change of system but simply to make sure that the needs of their region are better understood by the government. In all, however, 61% indicated that they would like to see some degree of change that would allow more decisions to be made in the region (Scale positions 3, 4 or 5) ... Scotland was most in favour of more regional decision taking with 71% wanting some change ...; Wales, however is only average in this respect."

This interpretation finds its way into the Report in the following form: ",.. 61 per cent. of respondents appeared to favour at least a moderate degree of devolution involving more *regional responsibility* for taking decisions." (para. 287).[2]

It is, however, equally true that in spite of the bias of the question above referred to, 61% of all informants were in favour of keeping the present system (Scale positions 1-3) whilst only 37% favoured a new system (Scale positions 4 and 5); that in every region, including Scotland (51% to 47%), a majority took this view; and that in Wales there was greater than average support for keeping the present system (63% to 36%). In all regions, either (2) or (3) was the most strongly supported option. In every region but the South-West, there was greater support for the "home-rule" option ((5)) than in Wales, and even in Scotland, this option received scarcely more support (23%) than in the South (21%) or East Anglia (20%). If one looks at the other option offering substantial devolution (option (4)), support is greater in the South (25%) and as great in the North West as in Scotland (24%), exceeding 20% in five other regions. If one combines options (4) and (5), Scotland (47%) is hardly distinguishable from the South (46%), not usually thought of as a hot-bed of home-rule activism. So much for the quantity of support for devolution. The quality of support is hardly more compelling. Of those interviewees assessed by interviewers as having a very or fairly good understanding of the questionnaires (3,819 of 4,892), 26% were in favour of option (3), 25% in favour of option (2) and 23% in favour of option (4), (Survey, p. 63). So far as education is concerned, total support for the first three options is greater among the better educated (62% of those of terminal age 20 or more; 66% of those of terminal age 17-19). So far as socio-economic group is concerned, there is a slight positive correlation between the height of the group and support for options (1)-(3) (Survey, p. 65). It might be considered significant that only 56% of interviewees in Wales and only 48% of them in Scotland answered "yes" to the question "is there a special office or organisation which helps to run Scotland-/Wales?". The Report itself recognises that this "tends to cast doubt on the quality of the support shown in the Attitude Survey

49

for further devolution" but again largely ignores this warning in the inferences it draws (paras 379-80). It would be remarkable indeed if the total of 47% of informants in Scotland who favoured the changes offered in options (4) and (5) contained none of the 52% who were ignorant of the existence of the Scottish Office and to the extent that these two categories do overlap it is surely right to question the value of expressions of desire for change. In fact, 38% in Scotland and 41% of those in Wales opting for option (4) were ignorant of the existence of the relevant office, whilst in relation to option (5) the proportions were 65% for Scotland and 53% in Wales (Survey, p. 83). Thus, if we take Wales, those who were knowledgeable and chose option (4) amount to 13½%; whilst those knowledgeable and choosing option (5) amount to 6%, a total of 19½% of informants who both knew of the existence of the Welsh Office and yet nevertheless wanted change. For Scotland, the figures are 15% for option (4) and 8% for option (5), a total of 23% knowing of the Scottish Office and yet wanting a new system of governing the region. This is not to say that all that is needed is some good p.r. by the Scottish and Welsh offices, nor yet that one can discount the views of those ignorant of the Offices. On the contrary, one might reasonably speculate that there exists a great deal of dissatisfaction with the present state of things — but that is far from establishing a widespread popular demand for devolution of a specific type which is, as I have tried to suggest in an earlier essay, merely one of a wide range of possible responses.

Such demand as there is should be further qualified. It is not an absolute demand. Whilst the majority of supporters of each of options (1) to (5) believed that devolution would make no difference to them personally, 28% of those opting for (4) and 34% of those opting for (5) believed they would benefit from it, only 3% and 2% respectively believing they would suffer (Survey, p. 96). Interviewees were also asked if they would maintain their preferences (a) if it meant that people in other regions would be better off and (b) if it meant that people in the home region would be worse off than at present. The data published by the Survey do not enable us to calculate the attitudes for supporters of options (4) and (5) by themselves (a good example of covert interpretation by the investigators) but they do reveal that for the 61% who support options (3) - (5), over half would abandon that preference if condition (a) were fulfilled and 5/6ths would abandon it if condition (b) were fulfilled. This is crucially important because it reminds us that the decision whether to devolve or not (and, if so, how) is not a matter of responding to a firm and settled public opinion at all, so far as the vast majority of people are concerned. Rather it urns necessarily upon expert judgement as to what the consequences of devolution would be, especially in relation to the dissatisfactions and discontents of the people.

Since the question of the establishment of popular assemblies in the regions has become a matter of party political significance, it is worthwhile remarking upon one other finding of the Attitudes Survey. Informants were asked:

"If (your region) had more say in running its own affairs, which of these three types of people would you like to be mainly responsible for taking decisions here, civil servants, people elected by those who live in the region, people appointed because of their special expertise?" Over Great Britain as a whole, the vast majority of informants divided fairly evenly as between elected representatives and appointed experts (48% and 45%). Experts were marginally *more* favourably viewed in Scotland (47%, 46%) and Wales (47%, 48%). It is to be noted that the question assumes that there is to be an extension of regional decision making and informants were asked simply to prefer, making that assumption. The answers do *not* indicate that 48% want elected assemblies (Survey, pp. 86-87). In this light, the views expressed in the Report, that "There is . . . the demand, not unanimous but substantial, for new elected assemblies in Scotland and Wales. And while there is not the same clear evidence of such a demand in the regions of England, it is argued by some ... that a latent demand exists" (para. 313), and that "In many quarters non-elected bodies are unpopular" (para. 315), whilst literally true, can be seen to give one a nudge in a particular direction not justified by this evidence.

The authors of the Memorandum of Dissent rightly take the point that these findings suggest that there is no case for treating Scotland and Wales much, if any, differently from the regions of England should greater devolution be instituted (para. 66). They do, however, take the surveyors to task for underplaying the evidence as to the strength of interest in devolution (para. 69). The basis for this criticism is Tables 55 and 56 of the Survey which show approval, strong or mild, for the propositions following:

"If regions had more say in the running of their own affairs:
   (a) the ordinary man could have more say in deciding what is done in the region (76%)
   (b) the needs of the people in the region would be looked

51

after much better (81%).

(c) things would be run more efficiently in the region (76%)."
The dissenters therefore conclude that "the idea of more devolution . . . is favoured by a substantial majority of people in all parts
of Britain as a means of increasing participation in government
. . ." (para. 70). This assumes, of course, that the only way in
which a region can have "more say in the running of its own
affairs" is by an extension of devolution. If this is so, it seems
impossible to reconcile the level of support here indicated (76-
81%) with that apparently indicated in Table 45 (only 61% for
options (3) - (5) inclusive, let alone the fact that options (4) and (5)
(the a"new system" options) enjoy the support of only 37%).
Thus either the Survey is not worth the paper it is printed on, or
the above assumption, that devolution is the only way of having
more say in the running of affairs in a region, is unwarranted. I
believe the latter to be the case. There are many ways other than
an extension of devolution in which the people of a region can
have more say in running the affairs of a region, all variants of
extending popular influence and control over central government in connection with the decisions which it and its servants
make in relation to a particular region. We should perhaps remind ourselves at this stage that the most popular of the five
options dealt with in Table 45 were (2) ("keep things much the
same as they are now but make sure that the needs of the region
are better understood by the government") and (3) ("keep the present system but allow more decisions to be made in the region")
both of which courses can be entirely accommodated by a more
sensitive local and regional administration of central government services, or even, perhaps, by an extension of the real decision-making powers of local authorities.

Discontent

The more reliable results of the Survey are those obtained in
response to the first part of the questionnaires dealing with the
desire for change and attitudes to government; more reliable simply because although the questions are to some extent leading,
they are less so than those relating to regional association and
devolution. There is very little complacency about the present system of running Britain (5%, Table 1, p. 1). 43% can see room for
small improvements and 49% think the system needs "a lot" or "a
great deal" of improvement. Table 17 (p. 20) gives the most

important clues as to this dissatisfaction. Offered five options (agree strongly or a little, disagree a little or strongly, don't know) in relation to various propositions, the following attitudes were evidenced:

1. "There should be more opportunity for ordinary people to get on to the council" — agree — 67%; disagree — 28%.
2. "The council should take more notice of the views of the people who live in the area" — agree — 91%; disagree — 7%.
3. "Most M.P.s are on the side of the man in the street and are always willing to listen to his views" — agree — 60%; disagree — 36%.
4. "It's too difficult for ordinary people to make their views known to the government about things that affect them" — agree 76%; disagree — 21%.
5. "M.P.s don't have enough power and influence on what decisions are made" — agree — 55%; disagree — 36%.

This table also offers us the opinions that only 22% think the local council, and only 30% think government, tells people enough about what it is doing.

The significance of these and associated findings escapes neither the Report nor the Memorandum. The Report identifies a clear demand for more participation and better communication, though it is a diffuse demand and it is not clear what specific action is called for (paras. 310-324). The authors of the Memorandum see the feeling of "powerlessness" as occupying the centre of the stage and being compounded of three distinct ingredients:

1. A "felt lack of communication";
2. A "felt lack of participation", much underplayed by the commentary in the Attitudes Survey; and
3. A large body of unresolved grievances, exacerbated, one might add, by despair, so far as a substantial minority are concerned, that their grievances will ever be anything but unresolved.

The Unasked Questions

Mulling over the Attitudes Survey satisfies me that there is a general desire for something different in government. I am far from convinced that it is an extension of intermediate level vertical devolution. I phrase that negatively because there is no sufficient evidence to the effect that more devolution of this type would not do the trick. We might have obtained some such evidence if we had asked different questions. Supposing we had offered informants the opportunity to choose between a new form of regional government in which there would be the same opportunities for participation as in local and central government at present; in which members took as much notice of people's views as do local councillors at present; in which lines of communication were as open as at present and in which members used their undoubted power and influence in the same way as at present. Suppose we offered them the choice between that, and a re-vamped, remodelled central government in the functioning of which they felt they had a substantial say; which informed the people about what it was doing; and in which their grievances were more effectively listened to and remedied; what, I wonder, would they choose?

Conclusion

I do not suppose for one moment that there is a negligible demand for regional government. I would think there is some; but I regard the Attitudes Survey as being quite unreliable as an indicator of its size and intensity. The latter is perhaps all-important. Nothing, including a failure to devolve, will work well if it fails to receive the acquiescence of the vast majority and that may mean that one cannot ignore even a small minority demand for devolution if that minority is sufficiently intolerant and determined. That, however, is a different matter and figures nowhere in the Report and Memorandum as a reason for devolving.

What I do suggest is that we do not have a sufficient justification for devolving simply in terms of popular demand or, indeed, in terms of the evidence of experts, most of whom supporting devolution have a clear interest in its extension. There remains the third possible justification, the use of various forms of devolution, among many other devices, in order to abate the discontent, remedy the grievances and dilute the dissatisfaction with government which is clearly established as a part of the political scene. This task may be more urgent than we think for there may well come a point when this widespread disaffection turns into an ineradicable cynicism. Proper enquiry may then reveal genuine and widespread support for radical changes in the system, generating forces which cannot be contained merely by adjusting existing mechanisms of government.

One final point. It is extremely unlikely that schemes for devolution motivated by party political advantage will happen, also, to cure the real ills. The physician must heal himself and since there is little evidence that he is even aware of the illness there is not much room for optimism, the less so now that the White Paper has appeared in all its nakedness.

APPENDIX A

The Brief provided by the Commission on the Constitution	*Section in which covered*

1. *Questions on the Theme of Participation*

What we need to know under this heading is the extent to which dissatisfaction arises from the following:-

  (a) The feeling that there is "too much government" and too little individual liberty.   II

  (b) The feeling that the "ordinary man" can play no part in the processes of government-that "We and They" situation. Does he want to play a bigger part and why doesn't he under existing arrangements?   II

  (c) Is the "We and They," situation a grievance directed not so much against the institution of government but at the big economic and other organisations outside government?   II

  (d) The feeling that nobody pays attention to the individual's grievances.   II

  (e) The feeling that there is too much secrecy about the decisions of government, whether central or local.   II

  (f) The feeling that everything is decided in London and that local and/or regional interests are disregarded.   II

  (g) Whether the desire for local decisions on "priorities" is stronger or weaker than the desire for equal quality in services.   V

  (h) The feeling that individual Members of Parliament have too little power and influence.   II

57

2. Questions on the Theme of Nationalism

(a) Does nationalism in Scotland and Wales add a different dimension or intensity to any of the demands in para 1?

IV

(b) What is the extent of the demand for independence (i.e. Commonwealth status) in Scotland and Wales?

IV

(c) How many in Scotland and Wales would want independence if it were clear that as a result they would be economically worse off?

V

(d) What proportion of people in Wales want the Welsh language to be:—
   (i) a compulsory part of the school curriculum?
   (ii) an equal alternative to English in the transaction of public business?

III

(e) How far are people more concerned with the trappings and symbols of nationalism than with the substance? (e.g. are they more concerned to have, say, special postage stamps as a symbol of nationalism than real independence as an expression of it?)

IV

*(f) Certain groups in Scotland already have close relationships with St. Andrew's House. Is it these groups who want more devolution—or is the demand for more devolution limited to those who do not have this close relationship?

—

*(g) Who would feel aggrieved if more decisions than now were devolved to St. Andrew's House? Scottish M.P.s? Those groups and individuals who are not part of the "Scottish Establishment"?

—

(h) How much is the demand for more devolution based on ignorance of the extent to which devolution already operates? Do people in fact want more devolution than actually exists as present?

IV

(i) Are there greater social, economic and cultural differences within Scotland (and Wales) than between Scotland (and Wales) and other parts of the United Kingdom?

III

---

* These two points could not be covered in this survey because they refer to tiny minorities in one region.

3. Questions affecting possible forms of devolution

(a) Are there social, political, cultural, racial and religious minority groups within regions (and within Scotland and Wales) which are more likely to be dominated and their interest adversely affected by regional majorities than by a United Kingdom majority?   V

(b) Devolution is often advocated so that regions can establish their own patterns of education and social etc. expenditure. Do people want variety or uniformity in the standards and type of, say, educational, medical and social services as between the different regions of the United Kingdom? Or is the main demand here coming from regions that feel themselves deprived in these respects and below the national average?   V

(c) In so far as there is a demand for more devolution, is it a demand for more devolution of power to local or regional administrators, or to local or regional elected bodies? Do public attitudes to government decisions differ according to whether the decision is made by an elected body or by officials?   IV

(d) Why do people want more devolution?   IV

(e) Is there any regional feeling akin to Scottish or Welsh nationalism? What is the difference between the feeling among, say, Yorkshiremen that they are Yorkshiremen, and the feeling among Scotsmen that they are Scotsmen?   III

APPENDIX B

TABLE 45 Degree of Devolution Chosen

Question 28(a) "For running the region as a whole, which of these five alternatives would you prefer?"

	Total	Area											
		North	Yorkshire	North West	West Midland	East Midland	East Anglia	South East	Greater London	South	South West	Wales	Scotland
Weighted base: all informants	(4,892)	(230)	(496)	(612)	(512)	(224)	(231)	(628)	(753)	(213)	(284)	(244)	(465)
	%	%	%	%	%	%	%	%	%	%	%	%	%
(1) Leave things as they are at present	13	11	16	8	15	12	16	14	16	11	20	15	6
(2) Keep things much the same as they are now but make sure that the needs of the region are better understood by the government	24	27	23	19	23	23	24	29	24	23	28	27	19
(3) Keep the present system but allow more decisions to be made in the region	24	26	24	30	26	26	17	21	24	20	20	21	26
(4) Have a new system of governing the region so that as many decisions as possible are made in the area	21	20	20	24	18	21	21	20	19	25	17	23	24
(5) Let the region take over complete responsibility for running things in the region	16	16	16	15	17	18	20	16	14	21	12	13	23
Don't know	2	1	1	3	1	0	2	1	2	0	2	0	1
Unweighted numbers of informants	(4,892)	(159)	(506)	(447)	(508)	(164)	(169)	(461)	(495)	(156)	(209)	(726)	(892)

Source: Kilbrandon Commission Report

NOTES

1. Kilbrandon's is not, of course, the only inquiry which purports to detect substantial popular demand for devolution. I can only suggest that other inquiries should also be closely scrutinised. Inspired by similar research in the U.S.A., I once conducted an attitudes survey in Northern Ireland which revealed that 60% of 80 subjects chosen at random approved or disapproved mildly or strongly (they could also hold no opinion) of the Polyastrian Brotherhood which did not exist.

2. The italicised phrase is not used in the survey commentary. The concept of "responsibility" certainly exaggerates the significance of responses in scale position 3 of question 28(a).

V WALES AND LEGISLATIVE DEVOLUTION
D. G. T. Williams*

Now I am not going to argue the question whether Wales is a nation, but I will say there are present in Wales — and no man with open eyes can deny it — conditions and circumstances which make it so unlike England that it ought to be dealt with differently from England. (James Bryce, 1892)[1]

Generalisations about a people are difficult to make and usually unsatisfactory, but it seems true that as one moves eastward and southward through Wales, the 'Welshness' of the people, though it undergoes subtle changes, persists. Despite divisions and gradations, there remain a strong sense of Welsh identity, a different way of looking at things and a distinct feeling that the needs and interests of people in Wales must be considered separately from those of people elsewhere in the United Kingdom. (Royal Commission on the Constitution, 1973)[2]

1. Introduction

The existence of a separate Welsh 'nation' has been asserted or disputed from time to time over the past hundred years. Some of the arguments have been as fanciful as those advanced at an earlier period to suggest that the Welsh had Trojan or Phoenician origins.[3] It is a difficult area to explore. As a background to a discussion of devolution it is perhaps sufficient to take note of Lloyd George's claim that no one can read the history of Wales for ten minutes 'without discovering that she had a separate national existence',[4] of the Royal Commission's assumption of 'the fact of nationhood' in relation to both Scotland and Wales,[5] and of a recent judicial observation that 'the Welsh are a nation — in the

*Fellow of Emmanuel College, Cambridge.

popular, though not in the legal, sense — by reason of Offa's Dyke, by recollection of battles long ago and pride in the present valour of their regiments, because of musical gifts and religious dissent, because of fortitude in the face of economic adversity, because of the satisfaction of all Wales that Lloyd George became an architect of the welfare state and prime minister of victory'.[6] The assertions of a separate national identity, whatever their validity, have become politically important in Wales as in Scotland by providing an emotional stimulus for regional government in the United Kingdom. Feelings of 'regional identification' certainly exist in several parts of England as well,[7] but the combination of nationalism and regionalism has dictated the emphasis of most constitutional proposals for federal or regional government — towards Scotland, Wales and, of course, Northern Ireland.

The modern political movements associated with the national identity of Wales date from the later nineteenth century and gained much of their initial impetus from the struggles over Home Rule for Ireland.[8] There has been talk of separatism, of federal government, of legislative devolution and of administrative devolution; there have been specific grievances (for instance, as to land, education, or the disestablishment of the Welsh Church) and more general complaints that Wales 'has too long been regarded as the Cinderella among the constituent nations of the United Kingdom';[9] and support for Welsh interests has come from within the major political parties as well as from home-based groups or parties such as Cymru Fydd and Plaid Cymru.[10] Private members' bills designed to secure extensive changes in Welsh government have been introduced on various occasions: the National Institutions (Wales) Bill 1892; the Government of Wales Bill 1914; the Government of Wales Bill 1922; the Government of Wales Bill 1954; the Government of Wales Bill 1967; and the Scottish and Welsh Parliaments Bill 1973.[11] The last of these measures was based on the Royal Commission's proposals for legislative 'devolution'; the previous two Bills by contrast were designed to produce something approaching the Stormont model of federal or quasi-federal government. Lord Ogmore said in relation to the 1967 Bill that he wished 'to extend the principle of federal government for the United Kingdom already in operation for Northern Ireland'.[12] There has been no suggestion in any of the proposed legislative measures, however, of anything more than federal government. Separatist proposals for an independent sovereign status for Wales, which were analysed and firmly rejected by the Royal Commission,[13] have been and are unlikely to secure either much support in Wales or much sympathy elsewhere in the United Kingdom. The underlying purpose of the various Bills, at least since 1914, seems to have been to move beyond mere administrative devolution. 'There has always been a certain amount of administrative devolution in Wales', said Mr Cledwyn Hughes in 1955, 'although I am always extremely suspicious of administrative devolution. I do not like the idea of bureaucracy being projected into the Principality without simultaneous answerability to an elected body there.'[14]

2. Administrative Decentralisation

Administrative decentralisation — as part of a deliberate policy of treating Wales differently from any defined region of England — has in fact been almost entirely a process of the twentieth century.[15] Education set the pace, from the Welsh Intermediate Education Act 1889 to the creation of the Welsh Department of the Board of Education in 1907; after some decades of pressures a Welsh Department of the Ministry of Agriculture was set up in 1919; and the provision under the National Insurance Act 1911 for a separate insurance commission for Wales was followed in 1919 by the formation of the Welsh Board of Health, which Ivor Gowan has described as 'the first significant devolution of the authority of a Government Department to Wales'.[16] But for twenty years after 1919 there was scarcely any further progress in decentralisation, despite the ravages of severe economic depression. The unemployed chose, in the words of the Royal Commission, 'to look fixedly, if resentfully, to the government in London, apparently seeing no prospect of salvation under a separate system of government in Wales'.[17] Welsh nationalism won little support at that time. Nonetheless the experience of the depression years left many people, Welshmen and others, with lasting scepticism about the capacity or the inclination of administrators based in London to deal sympathetically with the special problems of Wales. The grounds for this scepticism are vividly brought out by Alan Bullock in recalling how Ernest Bevin around 1934

'knew at first hand, as all too few Ministers and civil servants did, the physical desolation and the human degradation of industrial Wales. In London 8.6 per cent of the population was unemployed, in Oxford and Coventry, 5 per cent, even in Birmingham no more than 6.4 per cent. In Abertillery the figure was 50 per cent and in Merthyr Tydfil 61.9 per cent, although many of the men had already left to seek work elsewhere. To cross the Severn from southern England and journey across Monmouthshire and Glamorgan was to enter another world, a world of derelict communities and hopeless, listless faces. Every time Bevin made the journey he came back seething with anger at the complacency with which the rest of the nation and the Government could allow such conditions to continue.'[18]

The Second World War led to a renewal in administrative devolution in Wales. In 1940 the functions of the Welsh Board of Health were extended, there was a greater readiness during the war years to set up bodies to advise Ministers about the application of governmental policies to Wales, and by 1945 fifteen government departments had established offices in Wales. Some administrative devolution was inevitable in wartime and it was not by any means confined to Wales. But modest progress was maintained after the war, and efforts were made to improve departmental liaison, to enlarge the role of advisory bodies, and to provide the public with more information about government in Wales. At ministerial level, however, Wales suffered in comparison with Scotland. An attempt had been made to secure provision for a Minister with responsibility for Wales as early as 1892 in the National Institutions (Wales) Bill, and subsequent attempts were made in 1921, 1928, 1930 and 1939.[19] The office of Minister for Welsh Affairs was finally created in 1951, not in its own right but as a curious appendage to an established department of state. This inelegant compromise was abandoned in 1964 with the creation of the office of Secretary of State for Wales. The Welsh Office had now come into its own, headed by a Minister of Cabinet rank with exclusive concern for Wales. Between 1964 and 1972 the staff of the Welsh Office, who are with few exceptions based in Cardiff, increased from 225 to 990,[20] an increase which reflects the considerable expansion in functions assigned to the Secretary of State. But it is evidently difficult to estimate the degree of success achieved by the Welsh Office in satisfying local demands and local misgivings about the remoteness of government. The Royal Commission, in commenting upon both the Welsh Office and the older Scottish Office, said that they 'have undoubtedly been effective in securing additional benefits for

Scotland and Wales; but they appear to have made no very clear impression on the public at large, and the present system is criticised as not enabling them to develop a distinctively coherent set of policies for their respective countries and lacking in democratic accountability'.[21]

Emphasis upon the absence of adequate democratic accountability for the administration of the affairs of Wales has been a recurring theme in much of the political discussion and controversy since the later nineteenth century. 'Parliamentary congestion', claimed one Welsh Member of Parliament in 1902, 'has a great deal to do with the difficulty of obtaining time to discuss the affairs of a small country like Wales'.[22] It has been the practice in more recent years to allow some time for the discussion of Welsh affairs in the House of Commons during each session, but it is not surprising — especially since concern about centralisation and the weakening of democracy, as the Royal Commission recognised, is widespread throughout the United Kingdom[23] — that this concession to the 'national' interests of Welsh members is severely limited.[24] Legislation exclusively related to the affairs of Wales has been rare and principally concerned with linguistic and cultural matters. Public statutes in this century include the Welsh Church Act 1914 (providing for the disestablishment and disendowment of the Church of England in Wales), the Welsh Courts Act 1942, the Elections (Welsh Forms) Act 1964 and the Welsh Language Act 1967.[25] Recent private statutes include the Eisteddfod Act 1959, the Llangollen International Music Festival Act 1967 and the Welsh National Opera Company Act 1971. It is true that special provision for Wales in public statutes of general application has become increasingly common over the years,[26] but this practice inevitably limits both the time for discussion and the scope of legislative initiative in relation to Welsh needs. Perhaps the most important advantage allowed to Wales in parliamentary activities is numerical. Under the House of Commons (Redistribution of Seats) Act 1958 the minimum number of seats for Scotland and Wales is specified as 71 and 35 respectively, whereas if the same criteria were applied as for England the figures would be 57 and 31.[27] This over-representation appears to have been relatively uncontroversial up to the present time[28] — though one Member of Parliament complained in 1885 that Wales was 'a nation for the purpose of keeping Members which it was not entitled to as such'[29] — and, from a constitutional angle, it amounts to an unusual instance of preference being given in

67

the membership of a lower House to particular parts of a country with a unitary structure of government. A corollary of the Royal Commission's proposals for legislative devolution would be an end to such preferential treatment.[30]

3. *The Proposals of the Royal Commission*

The Royal Commission on the Constitution, which at the end of the day had thirteen members, considered numerous suggestions for the future government of Wales during the course of its deliberations from 1969 to 1973. Separatism and federalism were unanimously rejected,[31] and at the same time the Commissioners showed no apparent inclination to adhere to the *status quo*. Four separate schemes for change, one of which was set out in the Memorandum of Dissent (by Lord Crowther-Hunt and Professor A.T. Peacock), won some measure of support:

(a) A scheme of legislative devolution, which was acceptable to six of the eleven Commissioners who signed the Final Report: Lord Kilbrandon, Mr A.T. Davies, Sir Mark Henig, Dr J.B. Longmuir, Professor F.H. Newark, and Sir Ben Bowen Thomas.[32] There would be a transfer to a Welsh legislature, consisting of the Sovereign and a directly elected assembly, of responsibility for a number of specific matters which might include local government, town and country planning, housing, various environmental services, schools, health, forestry, and tourism. In exceptional cases responsibility might be divided between Parliament at Westminster and the Welsh legislature. Executive authority in relation to all transferred matters would be entrusted to Ministers appointed by the Crown and drawn from members of the assembly. A separate Welsh civil service would be created.

(b) A scheme of executive devolution, which was favoured by two Commissioners (Lord Foot and Sir James Steel).[33] Under this plan there would be a directly elected Welsh assembly with responsibility for subordinate policy-making and administration in accordance with the broader framework of policy and legislation adopted by Parliament and the central government in London. There would be similar assemblies for Scotland and for each of the specified regions of England. Executive authority would be vested in the assembly itself, and there would be a separate Welsh civil service.

(c) A scheme for 'intermediate level government', which was proposed in the Memorandum of Dissent,[34] allowing for seven democratically elected assemblies and governments — one for Scotland, one for Wales, and one for each of five English regions. The aim would be to transfer, at least in the long term, 'very substantial powers' to each of the assemblies and governments in the hope that this would help to 'restore' democracy in Britain and, in particular, enable Parliament to adapt itself to wider responsibilities both nationally and in relation to Europe.

(d) A scheme for a Welsh Advisory Council, which found favour with two Commissioners (Professor Harry Street and Mrs. N.K. Trenaman).[35] This would not involve devolution of legislative or executive powers. Instead there would be a directly elected council — replacing the existing Welsh Council — with the function of scrutinising central government policies and advising the Secretary of State for Wales and other Ministers about the application of such policies to Wales. The suggestion of a Welsh Advisory Council was also supported by a third Commissioner (Sir David Renton) in the context of proposing a similar body for Scotland equipped with some legislative as well as deliberative and advisory functions.

Underlying all four proposals is the assumption that the doctrine of Parliamentary Sovereignty should remain intact. The Royal Commission stated unequivocally 'that if government in the United Kingdom is to meet the present-day needs of the people it is necessary for the undivided sovereignty of Parliament to be maintained. We believe that only within the general ambit of one supreme elected authority is it likely that there will emerge the degree of unity, cooperation and flexibility which common sense suggests is desirable.'[36] That statement of principle, which echoes the sentiments which Dicey expressed in relation to Irish Home Rule,[37] would in itself explain the rejection of separatism and federalism by the Commission. Yet it is surprising that more space was accorded to separatism than to federalism.[38] Complete independence for Scotland or Wales has not been strongly supported in this century and it raises political implications of a nature which would certainly have fallen outside the competence of the Commission. Federal government on the other hand, albeit with minority support, has been seriously advocated from time to time since the later nineteenth century, and doubtless deserved better than the Commission's sweeping assertion that 'the United Kingdom is not an appropriate place for federalism and now is not an appropriate time'.[39] It is true that those who are prepared to speak of 'the arthritic articulation of federalism'[40] could refer to Dicey's denial of a 'federal spirit' in the United Kingdom[41] and to Balfour's assertion that the advocates of federal Home Rule were seeking to reverse the normal purpose of federation which, in his view, had hitherto 'always been the expedient by which disparate and scattered fragments are brought together in legislative union'.[42] Indeed, the Royal Commission's disapproval of federalism in the British constitutional context as 'legalistic' and 'strange and artificial'[43] was not unlike Balfour's condemnation sixty years earlier of 'these shadowy schemes of federalism',[44] and its stress upon the imbalance which would be created in a federation by 'the overwhelming political importance and wealth of England'[45] matched Balfour's reminder that England 'is, of necessity, from the mere accident of history if you will, by far the largest, by far the richest, and by far the most populous part of the United Kingdom'.[46] A fundamental objection to federalism which has been constantly raised since the days of Dicey and Balfour is its incompatibility with the sovereignty of Parliament; and the Commission noted with evident distaste that a federal government would require a supreme written constitution with special processes of amendment.[47] Again, as if to underline its orthodoxy in basic matters of constitutional law, the Commission more than once expressed its dislike of any prospect of judicial review of legislative action by elected bodies.[48]

4. *Federalism and Legislative Devolution*

In its Green Paper of June 1974 the Government went along with the Commission's rejection of federal government.[49] Nevertheless there is a measure of constitutional ambiguity in the 'next best' solution offered by a bare majority of the Commissioners who signed the main Report, namely the scheme for legislative devolution. In discussing the first Irish Home Rule Bill of 1886, Anson wrote that any future scheme for Ireland, 'if it is not to involve separation, must be on one of three lines, colonial, federal, or in the direction of an extension of local government'.[50] The Commission's scheme for legislative devolution does not purport to be separatist or federal; it certainly is intended to be something more than a mere extension of local government; and various factors — such as historical unity, geographical proximity, and the continued representation of Welsh members at West-minster — should deter one from exploring the possibility that in essence the scheme would result in a modified form of the status enjoyed by self-governing colonies in the later nineteenth century. Ambiguity arises because the Commission has incorporated many of the trappings of federalism into its proposals. Its scheme could fairly be described as a plan for 'semi-federal' or 'quasi-federal' government or 'federal devolution'.[51] Federal government is often accused of giving rise to an expensive and time-consuming multiplicity of representative and other institutions;[52] yet the Commission envisaged a separate Welsh legislature, a separate Welsh executive and a separate Welsh civil service superimposed upon a newly-fashioned structure of local government and subordinate to Parliament as well as closely interwoven with the Government and the civil service in London. One of the overriding problems associated with federal government is that of public finance, and the Commission — content that 'the constituent parts of the United Kingdom would not be straining to preserve an unrealistic measure of entrenched constitutional power'[53] — was confident that 'the sharp dissensions and protracted bargaining' which can occur over expenditure and revenue-raising in federal systems could be avoided;[54] but its own analysis of the practical possibilities under a scheme of legislative devolution for combining an integrated system of finance at national level with a considerable degree of regional independence, especially in matters of expenditure, cannot disguise the fact that this is a complex, speculative and relatively unexplored area of discussion.[55] Several of the so-called 'financial pitfalls of federalism'[56] may in practice be unavoidable, even in a scheme of government which falls short of creating a full-blown federation. It is, of course, an essential feature of federal government — even allowing for the notorious difficulty of formulating an acceptable definition of federalism — that the relationship between the central legislature and the regional legislatures is that of co-ordinate partners in a constitutionally-entrenched distribution of powers,[57] and with this in mind the Commission was anxious to assert that the transfer of powers under a scheme of legislative devolution would in no way detract from the ultimate and complete supremacy of Parliament. At the same time the Commission, encouraged by the experience in Northern Ireland up to 1972,[58] forecast that the power of Westminster would be invoked only in exceptional circumstances and that, for instance, a convention would arise that Parliament would legislate for Wales on a transferred matter only with the agreement of the Welsh government.[59] It is remarkable that such an interaction of law and convention should be contemplated in advance for an entirely new system of government, and in making its forecast the Commission came perilously close to proposing federal government without the courage of its convictions. In fact, one of the objections to legislative devolution was that it would introduce an element of rigidity into the relationship between Parliament at Westminster and the Welsh assembly. Those among the Commissioners who supported such devolution replied that this rigidity would be a source of strength in protecting the assembly 'from what would otherwise be an inevitable whittling away' of its powers through centralisation.[60]

In one major respect, however, the scheme for legislative devolution is fully consistent with the Commission's rejection of federal government. There is no provision for constitutional amendment, other than through a statute of the United Kingdom Parliament, and no provision for constitutional arbitration through the courts. What this means in effect is that the ambit of devolved powers and the scope of devolved government will ultimately be determined by the Parliament and the Government of the United Kingdom.[61] Something of the rivalry which the Commission sought to avoid in the context of public finance could emerge in relation to countless matters concerning the distribution of powers. A Welsh administration, which like its Scottish counterpart would have a national as well as a regional consciousness, would be unlikely to assume the role of a passive bystander or humble petitioner in questions of constitutional interpretation. The exclusion of the courts as the arbiters of constitutional disputes is explicit or implicit in the Commission's recommendations, and one is left to assume that these disputes will have to be settled through ordinary political processes. It would be unrealistic to underestimate the possibilities of conflict over the boundaries of power, whatever the attempted precision of a governing statute about legislative devolution; and it would be unwise to minimise the importance of securing a satisfactory mechanism for the settlement of conflict. Doubtless the political processes would suffice in many instances. But in some cases independent arbitration would surely be called for, and the appropriate forum would be a court of law. The Commission itself, with its questionable assumptions about 'the complete dissociation of the judiciary from matters of political policy',[62] may well have felt that overt recognition of the possibilities of judicial review would have added significantly to the 'federal' components of any of its schemes. The courts for their part, perhaps influenced by experience of the European Economic Community,[63] might respond to the introduction of legislative devolution by taking the initiative in asserting powers of judicial review — at least over actions of subordinate legislatures in the United Kingdom. Alternatively, if different views prevail, an arbitral role for the courts might at the outset be provided for by statute. In the Memorandum of Dissent, where a scheme for intermediate level governments throughout Great Britain is proposed, there is an interesting (though brief) discussion of the possibilities of constitutional review through the courts.[64] These possibilities are an added reminder of the difficulty of divorcing any scheme for legislative devolution from the familiar practices and problems of federal government.

5. *Special Treatment for Wales?*

There is obviously room for wide differences of opinion over the true nature of the scheme of legislative devolution set out in the main Report of the Royal Commission. But the scheme acquires a particular significance from the fact that it won support among the Commissioners *only* in relation to Scotland and Wales. For England there were varying degrees of support in the main Report for less ambitious schemes: executive devolution, the establishment of regional co-ordinating and advisory councils, and for co-ordinating committees of local authorities.[65] Those Commissioners who supported legislative devolution elsewhere in Great Britain — eight in the case of Scotland, six in the case of Wales — argued that it would do much to counter 'the physical remoteness from government which is felt in Scotland and Wales' and that it would have 'a revitalising effect on Scottish and Welsh life'.[66] Such arguments were advanced more confidently, as the numerical balance among the Commissioners indicates, in relation to Scotland. Apart from anything else, the Scots already possess a 'federal' prop in their separate system of law which 'produces a requirement for a considerable volume of separate Scottish legislation'.[67] But the six Commissioners who favoured the inclusion of Wales in the proposed scheme had this to say:

'While Wales has no separate legal system, it is a distinctive community with its own needs and interests and with a culture and language to preserve and foster, and there is scope for a substantial volume of separate legislation devised by the Welsh people to meet those special needs. Those of us who take this view believe that a generous measure of devolution, in recognition of the national identity of Wales and as a counter to the growing scale of government and spread of uniformity, would be more likely to strengthen than to weaken the unity of the United Kingdom.'[68]

Yet the growing scale of government and the spread of uniformity cannot in themselves be used as justification for treating Wales differently from the English regions. From the ordinary citizen's viewpoint, legislative devolution might appear to be increasing the scale of government by the introduction of an entirely new set of institutions between his local authorities and the central administration in London. His experience of the confusion sometimes resulting from the overlap of central and local government functions (for example, in the field of education) could lead to some apprehension about the possibility of a further blurring of the lines of responsibility under a scheme of legislative devolution. Nor would his apprehension be lessened by the knowledge that a Welsh assembly under the Commission's scheme would be in theory totally subordinate to London. If in truth legislative devolution is a disguised form of federalism or at least a major step towards the eventual acceptance of federal government, it might be preferable to recognise the realities at this stage. The institution of an elaborate federal-style government deprived of the essential attributes of federalism — 'a written constitution, a special procedure for changing it and a constitutional court to interpret it'[69] — could simply be a recipe for endless constitutional shadow-boxing. There is nothing to suggest that pre-1972 Stormont-style government, itself a fortuitous outcome of the struggles over Irish Home Rule, is capable of being adapted satisfactorily to meet the needs and demands of Wales and Scotland. In economic matters alone, especially in regard to natural resources such as oil and water, it could increase rather than reduce feelings of frustration and suspicion. Moreover many people might be discouraged from active participation in politics or in the public service simply because the dignity and status of government would suffer from its formal subordinate nature and its effective exclusion from the wider areas of policy and decision in

London and Brussels. Others with federalist or separatist aspirations might participate only in order to employ the new machinery of government as a manouvering device for securing their political objectives. The advocates of legislative devolution would doubtless discount such suggestions and argue that it is at least 'worth a try', but the danger of that approach is that it both underplays the immense constitutional changes involved in the Commission's scheme and overlooks the genuine possibility that a breakdown in legislative devolution could provide a favourable climate for separatism. Federal government might be bypassed altogether if semi-federal government failed. On the other hand it is arguable that federalism, if adopted from the beginning, could by its very entrenchment give a guarantee of greater stability in the formation and working of a new system of government. Variations in a system of legislative devolution would to no small extent emerge from the unseen processes of political adjustment and compromise; these processes would operate under federal government as well, but there would be additional open and controlling mechanisms through the availability of judicial review and the need to observe prescribed procedures — possibly incorporating a referendum — for constitutional amendment.

There is surely much to be said for a much closer examination than that undertaken by the Royal Commission into the possibilities of federal government. It may well be found that federalism, despite its well-known disadvantages, would be preferable to an unentrenched scheme of legislative devolution. The formulation of a federal plan would certainly provide a less ambiguous alternative solution to those proposals — such as the scheme for executive devolution or the idea of a Welsh Advisory Council — which seek to improve the process of administrative decentralisation rather than to secure the transfer of wide powers of primary legislation. Legislative devolution as much as federalism is fundamentally different in nature from executive devolution, but it would not appear so from the term itself or from the manner in which its advocates sometimes present it as little more than a new style of delegation from Parliament. Its implementation would presumably be achieved by an ordinary Act of Parliament rather than through more elaborate processes which would be or ought to be required for the institution of federalism. Its constitutional implications would be discussed and disputed by politicians and theorists, but largely obscured from the mass of people affected. The implications of federal government would be less difficult to assess, particularly because of the readily-available experience of English-speaking countries such as the United States, Canada and Australia.[70] A federal plan would be a more honest plan. It would bring home to everyone the radical and extensive changes which are envisaged. In particular for Wales, in its customary third place in the priorities of Home Rule, a clear-cut proposal for federal government might help to dispose of the assumption that what is appropriate for Scotland is also appropriate for Wales. It is not sufficient merely to speak of the distinct national identity of Wales. The real issue is whether the special position of Wales within the United Kingdom demands as drastic a solution as federal or semi-federal government. Such a solution may or may not be desirable, but its adoption should not be just an afterthought to developments elsewhere in the Celtic fringe.

6. *The Separate National Identity of Wales*

The distinct national identity of Wales can be explained largely on the basis of linguistic, cultural and religious factors. It was stated in the preamble of a statute of 1536 that the people of Wales 'have and do daily use a speche nothing like ne consonaunt to the naturall mother tonge used within this Realme',[71] and to a remarkable degree this language has survived and flourished to the present day. In claiming the existence of a Welsh nation, a Member of Parliament declared in 1892 that 'we are not only divided geographically, but also by the barrier of language'[72] and one of his colleagues stated a few years earlier that chiefly because of the language 'the Welsh are today the most distinct and homogeneous of the four peoples that make up the realm'.[73] Assertions of this kind reflect something of the emotions associated with the language throughout modern Welsh history. It has survived despite the dominance of English in law and administration and it continues to thrive with an unprecedented wave of official support and statutory recognition in the past ten or fifteen years.[74] The course of religious developments in Wales since the sixteenth century suggests that the regular use of Welsh as the language of worship — in the Established Church as well as among Nonconformist congregations — was 'the principal reason why Welsh held its ground so successfully in contrast to the much swifter decay of languages like Irish, Gaelic, or Cornish'[75] Many of the prejudices which operated against the Welsh language, especially during the nineteenth century, [76] have now disappeared or become subdued. But, although some of its supporters evidently feel that recent efforts to ensure the preservation of the language have been inadequate, there is room for genuine doubt and misgivings about the implications of bilingualism in such fields as education. A directly-elected Welsh assembly, under one of the schemes proposed in the Commission's Report, might provide a useful forum for debating and resolving some of the issues involved; but — in view of the fact that the majority of Welsh people are not bilingual — the outcome would be entirely unpredictable. The current policy of official benevolence, under a system of government from London combined with administrative decentralisation, may well be the most effective guarantee which supporters of the Welsh language can hope for in the immediate future. Simple democracy has its perils. There is certainly no convincing evidence to suggest that language and culture alone, in spite of their intimate association with the growth of Welsh nationalism and Welsh national consciousness in this century, can provide sufficient justification for the institution of a new and elaborate system of government along federal or semi-federal lines. Many people may already regret the extent to which the status of the language has become directly linked to political aspirations.

The justification, if any, for federal or semi-federal government should be based upon political and economic considerations. These considerations may be influenced but not dictated by racial, social, linguistic, religious, cultural and other factors. The realities of the Welsh situation have to be sought in the light of history, and Welsh history is quite different from Irish or Scottish history. The struggles for independence belong to the distant past — after 'the Britons were drove out of England, and retired among the mountains of Wales'[77] — and, after the success of Edward I's military campaigns leading to the promulgation of the Statute of Rhuddlan in 1284, the only serious rebellion was that undertaken by Owain Glyn Dŵr in the early fifteenth century.[78] Probably the most important single factor in cementing the peaceful integration of Wales into the English realm was the accession of a Welsh line of monarchs in 1485; and it was under the second of the Tudors that two statutes of 1536 and 1542, the significance of which has been underestimated in most books on English history, completed the process of unification.[79] Under the Union of 1536-42 the English system of law and administration was extended to Wales, though a separate system of Welsh courts — the Court of the Great Sessions[80] — was to last until 1830. The arbitrariness of the English-Welsh frontier, which was reflected until recently in the curious status of Monmouthshire,[81] was an indication of the lack of importance attached to its demarcation. Total integration was the order of the day. The Welsh people henceforth sent their representatives to the House of Commons in London and became more and more accustomed to English law and to English as the official language. Welsh students continued to attend Oxford and Cambridge universities, as they had done for many years, and Welshmen continued to seek their fortunes in London — not least in the legal profession. A Welsh university was not set up until the later nineteenth century; and, apart, from one or two short-lived bursts of activity in the Middle Ages, there have never been any Welsh parliamentary institutions. That Wales retained its separate identity after the Union is principally attributable to linguistic and economic factors, and the revival of active political consciousness is a product of relatively recent times:

> 'Down to the second half of the eighteenth century Wales was, economically speaking, a static and poor country with a primarily pastoral farming economy. It was governed by a landowning class which had now become completely anglicized, though the great majority of the population remained almost wholly Welsh in speech. The coming of the Industrial Revolution during the last decades of the eighteenth century led to a rapid transformation of the social and economic scene in the nineteenth century.'[82]

The Welsh population increased throughout the nineteenth century, and in the period of particular prosperity from 1851 to 1911 it grew from 1.2 million to 2.4 million.[83] English tended to be the language of business and industrial life, but Welsh clung on especially in rural areas. The new vitality in Welsh life, which must in part have resulted from the interaction of English and Welsh influences after so long a period of relative isolation, had its effect upon literature and the arts, music, and all forms of education. Politically Wales sprang into prominence because of the impact of a new generation of Welsh members of Parliament upon the British political scene at the turn of the century. Welsh nationalism flourished only sporadically in the new climate; but the reawakening of Welsh political consciousness was the stimulus for a process of administrative decentralisation which, after tentative beginnings, has grown apace in recent decades. From

78

the sixteenth to the nineteenth centuries Wales had formally been treated as part of England, and it is only in the last hundred years that the practice was adopted of referring to 'England and Wales' rather than 'England' alone in Acts of Parliament.[84] The first enactment to treat Wales separately was apparently the Welsh Sunday Closing Act 1881,[85] but it was not until 1967 that it was finally recognised that in law England did not include Wales.[86] Likewise Cardiff's official standing as the capital city of Wales is of very recent origin.[87] From a United Kingdom standpoint these are the bits and pieces of constitutional change. At the same time they illustrate the historical and constitutional differences between Wales on the one hand and Scotland and Ireland on the other. It is significant that not one of the Bills introduced in this century to secure separate Welsh legislative and executive institutions has hitherto attracted more than small minority support. The legal system remains the same for England and Wales; education in schools, colleges and universities is provided along substantially similar lines; and in economic, industrial and financial matters the two countries are inextricably linked.[88]

7. Selective Devolution

Why, then, should Wales be granted full-scale legislative devolution (or more) under a scheme which excludes England or any particular regions of England? The exclusion of England in itself creates an unsatisfactory imbalance in the scheme — something which is avoided in the plan advocated in the Memorandum of Dissent — and could in a very short time cause serious objections to the joint existence of a Welsh system of government and full Welsh representation in the United Kingdom Parliament. If legislative devolution is felt to be an answer to some of the problems of present-day government over the whole country, it would surely be preferable to have an evenly-spread system of regional government. But, if it is intended to be applied selectively as a recognition of separate national identities, the inclusion of Wales needs to be justified on very strong grounds. This is not only because of the close integration of England and Wales over so many centuries. It is also because the national identity of Wales, such as it is, reflects linguistic and cultural elements which do not in themselves present a compelling argument for substantial political change. It may be true, as the Royal Commission suggested, that the 'recent revival of interest in Welsh cul-

79

ture is the answer of a sensitive people to the pressures and disappointments of modern society'.[89] But the survival of the Welsh language and culture — especially when one bears in mind the cumulative effect of administrative decentralisation and revised official attitudes since the later nineteenth century — may already have been sufficiently secured by the new status accorded to the Welsh language in administration, in the law courts, in schools and universities, and in numerous other areas of cultural and social activity. Continued association with England within the United Kingdom is apparently something which the vast majority of Welsh people wish to retain; and, if this is so, the pre-eminence of the English language in Welsh affairs should be maintained — for obvious political, economic and social reasons, and also because the course of history has dictate that the cultural values of Welsh life are not easily separated from the cultural values of Welsh life are not easily separated from the cultural values of the United Kingdom as a whole. The maintenance of the delicate balance between the English and Welsh languages, which has evolved over the years, calls for continued moderation and understanding on the part of those responsible for government and administration. It surely does not require the institution of an elaborate system of legislative devolution.

The political and economic considerations relating to devolution also give rise to a considerable measure of doubt about the desirability of special treatment for Wales. Once again it should be stressed that an evenly-spread system of regional government is one thing, a selective system is another. The small size of Wales (just over 8,000 square miles) and its relatively small population (according to the 1971 Census, it was 2,723,596 or 4.9 per cent of that of the United Kingdom)[90] do not stand in the way of legislative devolution. Either in area or in population Wales compares favourably with many states or provinces within federations elsewhere in the world. Indeed, even among the independent nations, seventeen members of the United Nations at the end of 1968 had populations of less than one million and at least six others each had less than 150,000 people.[91] It could be argued with some force that politically and economically Wales would benefit under a separate system of government geared to cater for the special needs of the Principality and to act as a buffer against economic fluctuations and their often tragic consequences. The experience of the inter-war years, in particular, is not easily forgotten. Even the greater diversification of industry in more recent decades has not avoided acute problems of unemployment and depopulation.[92] Wales, as a peripheral part of the United Kingdom, has probably suffered more than most from the remoteness of government and excessive centralisation in the past. But, bearing in mind the Commission's statement that the rate of economic growth in Wales 'will continue to depend heavily on the level of economic activity in Great Britain as a whole',[93] it is questionable whether the appropriate course of action is to adopt a selective scheme of legislative devolution. An unentrenched Welsh government would, judging from the difficulties encountered by individual units within federations, have only limited scope for adapting central economic policies to the special needs or requirements of Wales: and it may be that it would achieve little more than is already possible under administrative decentralisation from London and restructured local government.[94] Perhaps above all, there is the very real danger that under the selective scheme proposed by the Commission the extent of Welsh influence in Whitehall and of Welsh representation at Westminster will be progressively reduced. The Commission itself recognised that, depending on the nature and degree of devolution to Wales and Scotland, it might be necessary to reduce the Parliamentary representation of the two countries below the level based on population, as was done in the case of Northern Ireland.[95] Yet legislation passed by a subordinate assembly in Wales or Scotland could be vetoed at the initiative of the Government and Parliament in London.[96] One might be forgiven for suggesting that the Commission, which at one point stressed that no advocate of federalism in the United Kingdom had produced a scheme satisfactorily tailored to take account of the dominant position of England,[97] has come up with a scheme which could emphasise that dominance more than ever. The critical economic and trading problems affecting the United Kingdom are matters of nation-wide concern: British participation in the European Economic Community will have to be regulated from London;[98] and the impact of multinational corporations and overseas investment raises issues which must of necessity be faced by the Government and the Parliament of the United Kingdom.

8. *Conclusion*

If it is decided at the end of the day that Wales must be treated differently from England, there are various possible courses of action: federal government; legislative devolution; or an extension of the present policy of administrative decentralisation. Federal government, for reasons indicated above, could for all its complications be preferable to legislative devolution and it might well provide the minimum guarantees which the Welsh would expect in exchange for reduced representation at Westminster. But neither federal government nor legislative devolution is likely to work satisfactorily under a selective scheme from which England and the regions of England are excluded.[99] In the absence of any viable scheme to include England, it might be wiser at the present time for Wales to accept an extension in administrative devolution.[100] The suggestion of an elected Welsh Advisory Council, for instance, has much to commend it, for it would be aimed at improving rather than revolutionising the existing system of government in Wales and could be valuable in ensuring that the special needs of Wales — in economic and cultural matters — are taken into account by those responsible in London and Cardiff. Even if more ambitious schemes are undertaken in Scotland,[101] it might be in the long-term interests of Wales to stand clear of the process of constitutional fragmentation. Such a policy may also be in the long-term interests of England and of the United Kingdom.

NOTES

1   H.C., 4th series, Volume 1, C-1067 (23 February 1892).

2   Report of the Royal Commission on the Constitution 1969-1973, Cmnd. 5460, para. 130, hereinafter referred to as the Report.

3   See Glyn E. Daniel, 'Who are the Welsh?' (Sir John Rhŷs Memorial Lecture, British Academy 1954), XL Proceedings of the British Academy 145.

4   H.C.,4th series, Volume 23,CC-1695-96 (30 April 1894). Earlier in the debate (which was on disestablishment), Sir M. Hicks-Beach had denied (at CC-1490-91, 26 April) 'that, historically, Wales has any claim to be considered as a separate nationality at all', stressing that Wales had never had a capital city, a separate government or a separate legislature. See G. Osborne Morgan. Welsh Nationality' (1888) LII Contemp. Review, 81.

5   Report, para 6. The Commission conceded at a later point (para. 326) that it is possible 'to argue endlessly' about the meaning of the word 'nation', and indicated that the factors to be taken into account in investigating alleged

national identity include geography, history, race, language and culture. In a similar but more confident vein, a Welsh MP in 1922 declared (H.C., Volume 150, C-936, 10 February 1922): 'Whatever may be the determining principle that decides the question of nationality, whether it be race, or territory, or common language, or community of sentiment and tradition, no one would dare to deny the right of Wales to call herself a nation . . . Wales is not a geographical expression' (Hugh Edwards).

6   London Borough of Ealing v Race Relations Board [1972] 1 All E.R. 105, 116, per Lord Simon of Glaisdale.

7   Report, ch. 7.

8   See Sir Reginald Coupland, Welsh and Scottish Nationalism: A Study (London: Collins, 1954), especially Part V on 'Wales in the Nineteenth Century'. See also, Owen Dudley Edwards, Gwynfor Evans, Ioan Rhys, Hugh Mac-Diarmid, Celtic Nationalism (London: Routledge and Kegan Paul, 1968).

9   H.C., Volume 116, C-2124 (3 June 1919) (Hugh Edwards).

10   See Report at paras. 347-53. On the background to Cymru Fydd (Wales of the Future), which was founded in 1886, see Neville Masterman, The Forerunner (The Dilemmas of Tom Ellis 1859-1899) (Wales: Christopher Davies, 1972); and Sir Reginald Coupland, op. cit. supra, at 227-28. On Plaid Cymru, which was founded as the Welsh Nationalist Party in 1925, see Coupland, Part VIII; and Memorandum submitted by Plaid Cymru to the Royal Commission — Commission on the Constitution, Minutes of Evidence I. Wales (HMSO 1970) pp. 29 ff.

11   See H.C., Volume 1 4th series, C-170 (on 1892 Bill); H.C., Volume LIX, CC-1235 ff (on 1914 Bill): H.C., Volume 153, CC-929 ff (on 1922 Bill); H.C., Volume 537, CC-2439 (on 1955 Bill); H.L., Volume 288, CC-702 ff (on 1967 Bill): H.C., Volume 868, CC-835 ff (on 1973 Bill.

12   H.C. Volume 288, C-702 (30 January 1968).

13   Report, ch. 12 ('Separatism').

14   H.C., Volume 537, CC-2449-2450 (4 March 1955).

15   For accounts of the development of administrative devolution in Wales, see Commission on the Constitution. Written Evidence I — The Welsh Office (HMSO, 1969) and Report Ch. 5. See also H.L., Volume 288, CC-709-10. (30 January 1968, Baroness Phillips).

16   Government in Wales (Inaugural Lecture 1965), (Cardiff: University of Wales Press, 1966), at 5.

17   Report, para. 349.

18   The Life and Times of Ernest Bevin: Vol. I — Trade Union Leader 1881-1940 (London: Heinemann, 1960), at pp. 539-40.

19   See the Written Evidence of the Welsh Office (supra, note 15), at para. 8; on the Bills of 1928, 1930, 1937. On the Secretary for Wales Bill 1921, see H.C., Volume 138, C-441 (18 February 1921) and H.C., Volume 150, C-929, (28 April 1922).

20 Report, para. 136.

21 Ibid, para. 385.

22 H.C., Volume CI, C-244 (17 January 1902) (Herbert Lewis). Some years later Asquith, when Prime Minister, had this to say (H.C., Volume XXI, C-1100, 15 February 1911): 'Wales is a very conspicuous illustration of the incapacity of Parliament — demonstrated by the experience of this Parliament, gigantic in size, and charged with the whole affairs of the Empire — to devote the requisite amount of time, attention and knowledge, to the local affairs of the constituent branches of the United Kingdom'. See also, H.C., Volume 116, C-1885 (3 June 1919) (Murray Macdonald) and H.C., Volume 537, CC-2441-42 (4 March 1955) (S.C. Davies).

23 See Report ch. 9 ('Dissatisfaction with Government in Great Britain'). 'There is no doubt', said James Griffiths in 1968 (H.C., Volume 770, C-276, 15 October 1968), 'that in the whole of this Kindom, as elsewhere in the world, there is something of a revolt against over-centralisation of power. This is one of the most important developments in our modern society.'

24 See Written Evidence of the Welsh Office (supra, note 15) at pp. 7-8 ('Wales in Parliament') and Report at paras. 139-40 and ch. 22 ('Regional Organisation Within Parliament'). Reference is made (at para. 1063) by the Royal Commission to the finding that, for example, 'there exists a feeling that the Welsh Grand Committee, of which much was expected when it was established in 1960, has been a relatively ineffective body'.

25 For a historical survey of the Welsh language in law and administration, see Report of the Committee on the Legal Status of the Welsh Language (the Hughes-Parry Committee); Cmnd. 2785 (October 1965) in Part II. The Welsh Language Act 1967 followed the recommendations of the Hughes-Parry Report. See Report, para. 133.

26 See Written Evidence of the Welsh Office (supra, note 15), especially at para. 18.

27 Report, footnote 1 on p. 31.

28 See the comments of Herbert Morrison, the Home Secretary, during the second reading debate on the House of Commons (Redistribution of Seats) Act 1944: H.C., Volume 403, CC-1614-15 (10 October 1944).

29 H.C., 3rd series, Volume 295, C-4 (4 March 1885)

30 Report, para. 1147. The number of constituencies for Northern Ireland is 12, whereas the same criteria as in England would produce 17 (see footnote 1, p. 31).

31 Report, Part V.

32 Ibid., paras. 1125-1153.

33 Ibid., paras. 1154-1173.

34 Cmnd. 5460-I, hereinafter called the Memorandum, especially at xii-xxii.

35 Report, paras. 1174-1183.

36 Ibid., para. 539.

37 See A.V. Dicey, England's Case Against Home Rule (London: John Murray, 3rd ed. 1887) at p.168: 'Under all the formality, the antiquarianism, the shams of the British constitution, there lies latent an element of power which has been the true source of its life and growth. This secret source of strength is the absolute omnipotence, the sovereignty, of Parliament.'

38 Ch. 12 on Separation extends over nearly nineteen pages; Ch. 13 on Federation covers just over nine pages.

39 Report, para. 539.

40 The Times, 1 November 1973, p. 19 (leading article).

41 See generally, Dicey's Law of the Constitution at Ch. 3.

42 H..C., Volume LIII, C-534, 30 May 1913 (during second reading of a Government of Scotland Bill). The Royal Commission said (at para. 526): 'No unitary state comparable to the United Kingdom has ever changed to federalism, with the exception of West Germany after the Second World War. The circumstances in that case were unique.'

43 Report, paras. 526 and 530 respectively.

44 H.C., Volume LIII, C-530, 30 May 1913.

45 Report, para. 531.

46 H.C., Volume LIII, CC-537-38, 30 May 1913.

47 Report, para. 527.

48 Ibid., para. 529 and especially para. 753.

49 'Devolution within the United Kingdom' (HMSO, 3 June 1974).

50 'The Government of Ireland Bill and the Sovereignty of Parliament' (1886) 2 LQR pp. 427, 442.

51. The term 'semi-federal' was used in the text of a leading article in The Times, 4 June 1974, p. 15 ('A Semi-Federal System'); the term 'federal devolution' was used in a debate in the House of Commons — H.C., Volume 116, CC-1837 ff — on 3 June 1919.

52 See e.g. Balfour in H.C., Volume LIII, C-538, 30 May 1913.

53 Report, para. 566.

54 Ibid.

55 See Ch. 15 ('The Public Finance of Devolution').

56 Report, para. 694.

57 See D.G.T. Williams, 'The Constitution of the United Kingdom' (1972B) CLJ pp. 266, 276.

58 Report, para. 1127.

59 Ibid., para. 1126.

60 Ibid., para. 1153 (c).

61 See especially ibid., paras. 764-67 (on Royal Assent to regional legislation).

62 Report, para. 529.

63 See the comments of Sir Leslie Scarman in 'Law and Administration: A Change in Relationship' (1972) Public Administration, p. 253, where he states (at p. 255) 'that the courts will have to assume the burden of interpreting and applying legislation which may be in conflict with statutes made by Parliament'. See also the report of a speech by Sir Leslie Scarman in The Times, 15 October 1973, p.4.

64 Memorandum, para. 308. For the Commission's proposals on the manner in which the Royal Assent might be withheld from provisional legislation, see Report, paras. 764-67.

65 Report, Ch. 25, which begins (at para. 1188): 'We are unanimously of the opinion that legislative devolution, even if it is applied to Scotland and Wales, as in each case a majority of us suggest, should not be applied to England or to the regions of England'.

66 Ibid., para. 1149.

67 Ibid., para. 1150.

68 Ibid., para. 1152.

69 Ibid., para. 527.

70 See Geoffrey Sawer, Australian Government Today (Melbourne Uni Press, 11th ed. 1973), especially Ch. 2.

71 See, Legal Status of the Welsh Language, Report of the Hughes-Parry Committee, Cmnd. 2785 (October 1965), para. 28.

72 H.C., Volume 1 (4th series), C-1104, 23 February 1892 (G. Osborne Morgan).

73 Stuart Rendel, M.P., 'Welsh Disestablishment' (1886) 50 Contemp. Review, p.777.

74 See Report, Ch. 5; Report of the Hughes-Parry Committee, supra note 71; Report of the Roderic Bowen Committee on Bilingual Traffic Signs, Cmnd. 5110, August 1972. See among legal cases relevant to problems of the Welsh language, Rv–(1848) 12 J.P. 789 and R v Thomas (1933) 24 Cr. App. Rep. 91 on juries; (see also H.C., Volume XXX, CC-414 ff (26 October 1911); and Viscount Simon, Retrospect (London: Hutchinson, 1952) at 60); Evans v Thomas [1962] 2 Q.B. 350 (electoral nomination papers); resulting in the Elections (Welsh Forms) Act 1964; R v Merthyr Tydfil JJ., ex p. Jenkins [1967] 2 Q.B. 21 (plea in court, involving consideration of the Welsh Courts Act 1942 but now to be read in the light of the Welsh Language Act 1967); Morris v Crown Office [1970] 2 Q.B. 114, C.A. (a contempt of court case, but see Lord Denning M.R.'s comments on the Welsh language).

75 Report of the Hughes-Parry Committee, supra note 71, para. 37. A Statute of 1563 authorised the translation of the Book of Common Prayer and the Bible into Welsh (ibid., para. 35). The special importance of religion in

86

Wales is apparent in the various parliamentary debates on disestablishment:e.g.'If I were asked to point to any spot in the world where Christianity had shown its most signal influence to civilise and elevate a people, I should point to Wales' (H.C., Volume I, 4th series, C-1036, 23 February 1892, Samuel Smith); 'The Church of England, with its stereotyped ritual and hierarchical constitution, was utterly unsuited to the genius of the Welsh people. In one word, it was too cold for an emotional people, too aristocratic and Bishop-ridden for a democratic people' (H.C., Volume 23, 4th Series, C-1505, 26 April 1894, Sir G. Osborne Morgan).

76 See especially the remarkable Report of the Commissioners of Inquiry into the State of Education in Wales: Accounts and Papers, 1847, conducted by R.R.W. Lingon, J.C.S. Symons and H.C. Johnson. For an account, see Sir Reginald Coupland, Welsh and Scottish Nationalism (London: Collins, 1954) at pp. 185-95: and see the comments in Report, paras. 115-16 on 'The Treachery of the Blue Books' ('Brady Llyfrau Gleision'). The Committee was apparently appointed because of a series of disorders in Wales in the first half of the nineteenth century.

77 R v Athos (1723) 8 Mod. 136, 88 E.R. 104, at 139, 106 (Kettleby, counsel for one of the defendants). See also, on the medieval or earlier periods: Lampley v Thomas (1747) 1 Wils. K.B. 193, 95 E.R. 568, at 198, 571 and 201, 573; R v Cowle (1759) 2 Burr. 834, 97 E.R. 587, at 850, 596; Campbell v Hall (1774) Lofft 655, 98 E.R. 848, at 689, 868. In 1894 (H.C., Volume 23, 4th series, C-1748, 30 April) Major Evan R. Jones said that the Welsh had 'planted Britain; and their history was old before English history began', a statement akin to that of Clement Davies in 1955 that 'we were here before anybody else arrived' (H.C., Volume 537, C-2508, 4 March 1955).

78 See Report, Ch. 5, especially paras. 109-12.

79 See David Williams A History of Modern Wales (John Murray, 1950), Ch. 3; Report para. 113; and H.C. Volume 23, 4th series, C-1704, 30 April 1894, when Balfour referred to the Union, 'which I confess I had never heard of before'.

80 See W.R. Williams, History of the Great Sessions of Wales 1542-1830 Together with the Lives of Welsh Judges (for private circulation, 1899); H.C. Volume LIII. CC-86 ff. 27 May 1913 (Sir D. Brynmor Jones on Welsh judges up to 1830).

81 See the explanation of Asquith at H.C., Volume 23, 4th series, C-1457, 26 April 1894: 'The district that now constitutes the County of Monmouth is part of what was anciently called the Welsh Marches. It was created into an English county, in so far, that is to say, as it ever has been an English county, — in the reign of Henry VIII, but it has always remained what it was from the first, predominantly Welsh in the habits, the sentiments, and the general character of the people.' See now in Local Government Act 1972, s.20(7), Sched. 4: and S.A. de Smith, Constitutional and Administrative Law (London): Penguin Books, 2nd ed. 1973), at p.673.

82 Report of the Hughes-Parry Committee, supra note 71, at para. 39

83 Report, para.123

84 See the Wales and Berwick-on-Tweed Act 1746, as amended by s. 4 of the

Welsh Language Act 1967; Nicol v Verelst 2 Black. V. 1277, 96 E.R. 751 at 1287, 755. See the comments of Morgan Lloyd M.P. in H.C., 3rd series, Volume 294, C-1961, 3 March 1885.

85 Commission on the Constitution, Written Evidence I, The Welsh Office (HMSO 1969) at para 2.

86 Welsh Language Act 1967, s. 4.

87 In 1892 a Welsh M.P. (Samuel Smith) could say: 'It is a common saying that Liverpool is the capital of Wales, because containing a larger body of Welsh citizens than any other city in the country' (H.C., Volume 1, 4th series, C-1039, 23 February 1892).

88 See Report, paras. 123-25.

89 Ibid., para. 356.

90 Ibid., para. 108. In 1914 E.T. John said in the House of Commons (H.C., Volume LIX, CC-1235-38, 11 March 1914): 'As regards the numerical strength and economic competence of Wales to undertake the responsibilities of self government, I would only remind the House that its population is greater than that of Norway and Cape Colony, and only slightly, if at all, less than that of Denmark, while it is more than three times that of Maine'.

91 S.A. de Smith, Microstates and Micronesia (Problems of America's Pacific Territories and other Minute Territories) (New York Univ. Press, 1970), at pp. 5-6.

92 Report, para. 124.

93 Ibid., para 125. In 1969 Sir Keith Joseph (H.C., Volume 782, C-345, 22 April) said that it would be ruin for Wales 'if she were economically separated from Britain'.

94 See the Local Government Act 1972. See also, The Reform of Local Government in Wales, a Consultative Document (HMSO, Welsh Office 1971).

95 Report, para. 815.

96 Ibid., paras. 764-67.

97 Ibid., para. 531.

98 On the Common Market, see Bryn John and others, The Common Market and Wales (Llandysul: Gomer Press).

99 But see the alternative scheme of intermediate local government set out in the Memorandum of Dissent.

100 See Ivor Gowan ('What Wales Would Lose under Kilbrandon Proposals') in The Times, 22 April 1974, p.14.The President of Plaid Cymru wrote in reply in The Times, 25 April 1974, p.17. See also the comments of the Welsh Council on the Kilbrandon proposals, reported in The Times, 15 June 1974, p.3.

101 Especially as a result of Scottish Nationalist success in the General Election of early 1974: see The Times, leading article of 27 February 1974, p.19; Max Peloff on 'Scotland, Wales and the Constitution' in Daily Telegraph, 12 March 1974, p. 16.

VI DEVOLUTION OF GOVERNMENT IN BRITAIN — SOME SCOTTISH ASPECTS

A. W. Bradley*

Questions of centralisation and decentralisation, delegation of decision-making and controls arise in all large human organisations. Public and private organisations alike have to set the economies of scale against the danger of bottle-necks at the centre, the encouragement of local initiative against the superior responsibilities of the centre and so on. The machinery of government, however, faces both these internal problems of management and co-ordination and also, to a much greater degree than private organisations, external problems of public accountability, democratic control and political support. In the late 1960s, the most prominent change in the organisation of British central government was a re-grouping of governmental functions which led to the appearance of five mammoth departments (Defence; Foreign and Commonwealth; Health and Social Security; Environment; Trade and Industry). Probably not all the changes were fully justified: as R.G.S. Brown has commented, "there is no simple relationship between administrative functions and the focal points of ministerial responsibility".[1] Certainly they did not solve all problems of delegation and management within a government department, for example, the problem of how to permit the local exercise of administrative discretion within a centralised bureaucracy.[2] Indeed, the size of the new organisations accentuated problems of delegating administrative responsibility, as evidenced by the inquiry into the collapse of the Vehicle and General Insurance Company.[3]

One of the aims of the re-grouping was to provide Ministers with the opportunity for "greater openness in government, and more responsiveness to the needs and wishes of the community

*Professor of Constitutional Law, University of Edinburgh.

and of individuals".[4] While the functional principle was emphasised as the basis for allocating responsibilities within Whitehall, with the aim of matching the organisation to suit the promotion of policy, it was accepted that there might be strong reasons for moderating the application of the functional principle. "Thus the functional principle does not invalidate the existing pattern whereby Scotland and Wales are treated separately,"[5] said the 1970 White Paper on the reorganisation of government. In fact the opportunity was taken at the 1970 reorganisation of transferring additional functions (child care, and the urban programme) to the Welsh Office but no changes were made in Scottish Office functions.

On the basis of the Report of the Fulton Committee on the Civil Service in 1968, and the 1970 White Paper it would seem that official thinking about the organisation of government before 1974 was not primarily concerned with geographical decentralisation and was content to accept Scotland and Wales as exceptional cases. Indeed, one of the best recent studies of the administrative process in Britain (written by a Scot who had himself worked in the civil service before becoming an academic) makes no reference whatever to geographical devolution.[6] In fact the larger departments have individually given much attention to maintaining schemes of regional and local offices to discharge their own functions. The emergence of regional economic planning in the mid 1960s led to a structure of official Regional Economic Planning Boards which are now chaired in England by the regional officers of the Department of Environment; and the Department of the Environment since 1971 has delegated certain highways, town planning and housing functions to its regional offices. But even within the Department of the Environment no integrated regional structure has yet been established, and the reorganisation just mentioned left the Department with no less than *eleven* separate regional organisations.[7] Central government as a whole, as opposed to individual departments, has not actively concerned itself with regionalisation except during the Second World War.[8] The reforms of local government in England, Wales and Scotland were carried through without regard to regionalisation of the activities of central government. The Redcliffe-Maud Report for England recommended eight provincial councils to bring together local authorities for the purpose of regional planning, but these have not been created; the Wheatley Report for Scotland, while recommending that the upper-tier in the new local government system should be styled regional authorities, dismissed summarily the idea of an all-Scotland elected assembly.[9]

With the political advance of the nationalists in Scotland and Wales, the publication of the Kilbrandon Report, the oil-based excitement in Scotland, and the effect of British membership of EEC in stimulating a fresh look at the structure of British administration, the issue of geographical devolution of government within Britain can no longer be avoided.

Hitherto, official thinking has professed to ignore the political dimension of Scottish administration and to rely on the yardstick of efficiency. As Sir Edward Bridges, then Permanent Secretary to the Treasury, said in 1953, "In the past the aim has been to secure the most efficient administration, it has not been to secure separate administration, whatever the price which has to be paid in loss of efficiency."[10] Nearly twenty years later Sir Douglas Haddow, then Permanent Under-Secretary at the Scottish Office told the Commission on the Constitution, concerning the transfer of functions from British departments to the Scottish Office, "on every occasion within government the question is looked at whether a particular development would be better handled as a Great Britain matter or as separate Scottish and English ones without any preconceived notions about the decision to be reached."[11]

Terminology

French legal writing distinguishes between *déconcentration*, a technique of organisation by which powers of decision are delegated to officials within the same hierarchy, and *décentralisation*, by which powers of decision are conferred on agencies and organs outside the central hierarchy.[12] It suggests an important theoretical assumption about the origin of governmental power that traditionally legal textbooks in France discuss local government under the heading of *décentralisation*; one even gives the example of a university faculty as an example of decentralisation.[13] The terminological distinction between deconcentration and decentralisation is not often found in English usage[14] but instances both of deconcentration and decentralisation are found in Britain. Thus (a) legislation may transfer powers from central government to an agency outside the departmental hierarchy (decentralisation) and (b) there may also occur (whether by legis-

91

lative or administrative means) delegation of powers within the departmental hierarchy (deconcentration). French writers tend to emphasise formal legal factors, for example the requirement that a decentralised agency has a distinct legal personality. In British practice, ministerial responsibility is more likely to be the criterion: as the Gilmour Committee on Scottish Administration said in 1937, in recommending the abolition of the last surviving Scottish boards, "the responsibility of the Minister to Parliament is inconsistent with any measure of independence (even if only apparent) in any Department for which he speaks."[15] Thus in Britain, one reason for "hiving-off" an activity to a specialised agency is to enable it to be exercised without the usual constraints of ministerial responsibility.

In current English usage, devolution has no precise meaning. According to the International Encyclopedia of the Social Sciences, devolution, as used by the English, "generally is equal to the French *décentralisation* but occasionally embraces *déconcentration* as well".[16] In the Kilbrandon Report, devolution is described as "the delegation of central government powers without the relinquishment of sovereignty" (para. 543). On the Kilbrandon analysis, this description excludes federalism but otherwise it leaves open such matters as the method of delegation, the constitutional or legal status of the delegate, the extent of retained control which might be consistent with delegation, and the problem of whether a power continues to be a "central government power" once it has been vested in a local or regional agency. On this last point it needs to be remembered that devolution may in some contexts refer to the *process* of devolving powers and in others to the *state of government* brought about after powers have been devolved.

Not surprisingly, the word devolution is rarely used in the Kilbrandon Report without a qualifying adjective: in particular, three forms of devolution receive attention, legislative devolution (described in Chapter 17 and defined at paragraph 734), executive devolution (Chapter 18, paragraph 827) and administrative devolution (Chapter 21, paragraphs 978 and 1022). Devolution in all these senses covers a very wide range of governmental structures. As used in the Report devolution includes measures both of decentralisation and deconcentration. Later in this paper, it will be suggested that administrative devolution is a misnomer, since the forms of government if refers to can scarcely be regarded as devolution at all. For the moment it is sufficient to say that the present Scottish Office system is based on the vesting of a good many diverse powers within a central government department (more accurately, a group of departments) created for a well-defined geographical area; although most of the administrative work of the Office is carried on within Scotland, the Ministerial team at the head of the Office is responsible to the U.K. Parliament for all the activities of the Office. Where powers of central government relating to Scotland are not vested in the Scottish Office, they are exercised by the appropriate British or U.K. department, in which case the British Minister is responsible to Parliament for both the English and Scottish affairs of the department. If in the latter instance, powers are delegated departmentally to the Scottish Controller of the British department, this is a clear instance of deconcentration. The Scottish Office however is not easy to classify in terms either of decentralisation or deconcentration.

To take the example of education (other than the universities), which is one of the most characteristic Scottish Office functions: so far as the English Department of Education and Science is concerned, Scottish education may be said to be decentralised since it forms no part of the English Department's responsibilities, nor indeed has it ever been part of those responsibilities. But so far as the Scottish Education Department and its place within the hierarchy of U.K. government are concerned, where is the decentralisation or the deconcentration — apart from the fact that most of the staff in the Department work in Edinburgh? An element of deconcentration would arise only if, say, officials in the Department were freer of ministerial control than their counterparts in England or if, say, Treasury control of Scottish educational expenditure were less stringent than Treasury control of English educational expenditure. Whatever may happen in practice, there is nothing to support the view that either of these situations is intended to exist. On this line of reasoning, the Scottish Office system demonstrates neither decentralisation nor deconcentration but merely a 'parallel' method of organising the work of the central government in relation to one geographical area of the U.K. Of course, if the Scottish Office system had *not* evolved, there would not be a much greater demand for measures of decentralisation or deconcentration in matters of Scottish administration. It is to aspects of that evolution that I now turn.

The Structure of Scottish Government

In the Union agreement of 1707, elaborate assurances were given for the continuance of certain Scottish institutions, primarily the legal system and the church, and for the maintenance of Scottish representation in the new Parliament of Great Britain. These assurances were the price paid for the suppression of Scotland's separate political and parliamentary existence. But the framers of the Union gave little apparent thought to the domestic administration of Scotland. William Ferguson has referred to "the dismantling of one system of government in 1707 without care being taken to provide an adequate replacement".[17] The abolition of the Scottish Privy Council in 1708 left a vacuum in government which has since been filled by a variety of expedients. The present Scottish Office system was established before the Second World War. It is not necessary to give more than the barest outline of its evolution here.[18]

For much of the 18th and 19th centuries, the visible entrenchment of the Scottish legal system and the need for a link between that system and the central government of the U.K. led to the Lord Advocate occupying the primary role in Scottish politics and government. When in the 19th century, the demand upon central government for social action became stronger, much use was made of *ad hoc* Scottish boards, whose responsibility to the Westminster parliament was neither close nor well-defined. Scotland is still served by some public corporations not found elsewhere in Britain (for example the Crofters Commission, Highlands and Islands Development Board, Mental Welfare Commission, Scottish Special Housing Association, Red Deer Commission, and the Commissioners of Northern Lights) and more are promised arising out of the development of oil.[19] But for most purposes of domestic administration, between 1890 and 1940 the former reliance on Boards gave way to the Scottish Office and local government system. In 1937, the Gilmour Committee on Scottish Administration, having been appointed to consider what organisational changes should accompany the physical move of Scottish administrators from Whitehall to new accommodation in St. Andrew's House at Edinburgh, recommended the abolition of the last surviving Scottish boards, and the vesting of their powers in the Secretary of State for Scotland. The Committee based their recommendation on the necessity for there to be ministerial responsibility to Parliament for every action of government: "the seeming independence of the Boards is ... illusory".[20]

These recommendations, implemented in the Reorganisation of Offices (Scotland) Act 1939, explain why the official guidebook to Scottish administration states: "The constitutional relationship between Parliament and the work of administration is the same in whatever part of Britain the latter is carried on."[21] By something of a paradox, the creation of the present structure of the Scottish Office marked both an abandonment of Scottish historical forms and also a physical move to enable day-to-day administration to be carried on in Scotland. (At an earlier date, a proposal to abandon the ancient forms without the physical move had been opposed by Scottish M.P.s.)[22] Yet for the Gilmour Committee, it was an important part of the new structure that the Scottish Office should be 'departmentalised' in a manner unlike other British departments: each of four departments within the Scottish Office was to have its own Permanent Secretary with direct access to the Secretary of State, and the Permanent Under-Secretary at the Scottish Office was to exercise an advisory, supervisory and co-ordinating role. Apart from the fact that this departmentalisation provided an evolutionary link with earlier forms of administration, it allowed the functional basis for organising government to be applied within the geographical limits of Scotland. It also facilitated functional links between the equivalent English and Scottish departments. These links have always been important in U.K. policy-making and budgetary procedures and have acquired an added significance with the more recent development of centralised methods of managing the U.K. economy. Today there are five departments within the Scottish Office: Education; Home and Health; Agriculture and Fisheries; Development (formed in 1962 and anticipating the creation of the English Department of the Environment by almost ten years); and Economic Planning, formed in 1973,[23] as well as various centralised Scottish Office services, for example the Solicitor's Department. While the Secretary of State retains undivided responsibility for the whole Office, detailed responsibilities for the various departments are shared between his supporting Ministers. The ministerial arrangements, in fact, are not unlike those adopted in the mammoth departments created in the late 1960s. It may be added that the Lord Advocate's Department and the Crown Office are not part of the Scottish Office: for them the Lord Advocate is personally responsible to Parliament.

As well as dealing with the internal organisation of the Scottish Office, the Gilmour Committee also popularised the notion of the Secretary of State as "Scotland's Minister": "Our evidence shows that there is an increasing tendency to appeal to him on all matters which have a Scottish aspect, even if on a strict view they are outside the province of his duties as statutorily defined ..."; "there is a wide and undefined area in which he is expected to be the mouthpiece of Scottish opinion in the Cabinet and elsewhere".[24] This notion, or convention, has a special significance for it relates to the second leg of Scottish administration, namely the British or U.K. departments which operate in Scotland to administer matters not within the direct responsibility of the Secretary of State. Since the days of the Gilmour Report, the central government has learned to give greater care to the adequate manning of the Scottish outposts of these departments.[25]

In 1954, the Balfour Commission on Scottish Affairs endorsed the main features of the Scottish Office structure and discovered few additional functions suitable for transfer to the Office from British departments. While the Commission advanced the principle that "in the absence of convincing evidence of advantage to the contrary, the machinery of Government should be designed to dispose of Scottish business in Scotland"[26], it accepted that one way of achieving this was for a British department to make suitable arrangements for enabling decisions to be made in Scotland; thus in the view of the Balfour Commission, the Scottish Office system was not the only method of enabling Scottish business to be disposed of in Scotland. For when it came to considering the allocation of functions between the Scottish Office and British departments, the Commission applied a different burden of proof, holding that any proposal to divide geographically the ministerial responsibility for a function currently vested in a British minister "would require to be supported by clear evidence that (a) distinctive Scottish interests would be better served and (b) the interests which Scotland has in common with the rest of the U.K. or Great Britain would not suffer".[27] By these cautious words, the Commission held fast to the two legs of Scottish administration formed respectively by the Scottish Office and the British departments.

After 1945, while social insurance and poor law functions were taken from the Scottish Office to enable the present social security system to be established in Britain, the general trend was for the Scottish Office to acquire additional functions, a trend indirectly reinforced by the creation of the Welsh Office on similar lines in 1964. Official thinking has adhered to the position that the division of functions between British and Scottish departments must be decided pragmatically according to the merits of each particular proposal.[28] According to the Balfour Commission in 1954, the functions vested in the Secretary of State were those which brought central government into relationship with local authorities, or which affected law and order, or which arose from the recognition of distinctive Scottish conditions; whereas responsibility for trade, industry and economic conditions generally remained with British ministers. In 1957 Sir David Milne, then Permanent Under-Secretary at the Scottish Office, recorded a "definite and increasing tendency" to assign to the Secretary of State matters on which there was a distinctive Scottish tradition or body of law or where Scottish conditions were notably different from those in England; but he admitted that the river of administrative development had flowed erratically and had not ceased to flow.[29] In 1973 the Kilbrandon Report found that in recent years the Scottish Office had become much more closely concerned with matters of economic development, whether or not these functions came under the direct responsibility of the Secretary of State.[30] In line with the official evidence given to the Commission, the Kilbrandon Report could see "only very limited scope" for adding to the executive functions of the Scottish Office.[31] In particular, the Commission did not recommend the vesting of trade and industry functions in the Secretary of State.

A convenient summary of the position was given in the Kilbrandon Report: "The main feature of the existing system of administrative devolution to Scotland and Wales is that in each country the Secretary of State has in certain subjects full responsibility both for the formulation of policy and for its execution, and in others a more general responsiblity for representing his country's interests to departmental Ministers individually and to Ministers collectively in the Cabinet."[32]

Criticisms of the Present Structure

If as a system Scottish administration has developed in a pragmatic manner to meet the special needs of Scotland, combining what might be thought to be the best of the two worlds of Whitehall and St. Andrews House government, why does it seem to receive so little support? and why, particularly if it is accepted that Scotland has received a reasonable share of public expenditure in recent years, is it apparently on the brink of being radically reorganised? Notably, further development of Scottish and Welsh Office administration was not one of the options currently presented by the Government in 1974 for public discussion.[33]

In the first place, the allocation of functions between British and Scottish departments is complex and difficult to justify on any simple theory of regional government. Possibly the only easily understood aspect of the present division of functions is that local authorities in Scotland have no dealings with Whitehall departments but only with Scottish Office departments. In a recent study of Scottish administration, Kellas remarks, "One could argue that the range of functions exercised by the Scottish Office is both too great and too small" — too great, since the varied collection of subjects within the Scottish Office is too great for collective political direction, too small, since there are "curious gaps" in the Scottish Office's powers, where responsibility is shared with British departments.[34] In Kellas's view, these gaps arise notably in relation to education, power, transport, economic development, health and social security. Possibly employment and agriculture are stronger candidates for inclusion in this list than either education or social security.[35] But Kellas is right to describe transport as "a confusion of functional and geographic administration"[36] and suggests with reference to criteria such as "distinctive Scottish conditions", that attempts to define what is predominantly "British" and what is predominantly "Scottish" have led to "notable impasses and anomalies".[37] Professor Mitchell has commented, "The real departmental responsibilities of the under-secretaries of State remain hidden under legal formalism so far as the public goes."[38] More fundamentally, he has argued against the entire concept of the Scottish and Welsh Offices in the conditions of modern government.[39]

Secondly, as with many other aspects of British government, the secrecy of the decision-making process makes it virtually impossible for external commentators to allot praise or blame.[40] When Sir Douglas Haddow was asked by a member of the Commission on the Constitution to give one or two instances where the Scottish Office had supported a British department in seeking the necessary authority for new developments (presumably from the Treasury or a Cabinet committee), he replied:

"Frankly, I am not sure how proper it is for me to do so, but examples would be things like the location of the prototype fast reactor at Dounreay and various common exercises between the Scottish Office and the Ministry of Technology. The Scottish Office finger would usually be in the pie. It would be wrong of us to flaunt it, and I would like to be excused from explaining how this exercise works, but it does work."[41]

This answer justifies the comment, "Scottish Office policy initiatives, if they exist, are by the nature of things subterranean, if not completely invisible."[42] The recent development of Scottish Office concern for the economic state of Scotland, without being permitted to exercise trade and industry powers, is a likely recipe for confusion and disappointed expectations. Again, in Scotland as in England, the existence of public corporations and advisory bodies seems to make the problem of an over-secretive governmental system worse rather than better.[43]

Thirdly, while the Scottish Office does have some scope for administrative initiative, however ill-defined, the Office remains part of a single governmental system and runs a constant risk of being seen as no more than a distant outpost of Whitehall. The Scottish Office system may well illustrate the rigidity and not the flexibility of the British governmental system.[44] According to the Kilbrandon Report the Scottish Office has a marginal ability to re-allocate financial provision made for its departments, but the weight of the evidence is that this ability is of minimal importance[45] which explains the categorical statement by the Scottish Office that expenditure by the Scottish departments is controlled in the same way as expenditure by Whitehall departments.[46]

Fourthly, the greater the emphasis on the Scottishness of the system, the greater the gap revealed between administrative power and political control. When asked whether he would agree that devolution of administration is the shadow and not the substance of power, Sir Douglas Haddow replied: "It ought to be; I am not sure that it always is."[47] While the system allows for some administrative initiative to be taken by Scottish departments, how often is this the result of political pressure? When Sir Douglas Haddow was asked how sensitive Scottish administration was to the will of the Scottish people, he replied: "I would find it easier to answer that question if somebody would tell me how to ascertain the will of the people of Scotland."[48] He clearly did not regard the 71 Scottish M.P.s at Westminster as serving this purpose. The lack of a solid political base for Scottish administration brings into question the expression "administrative devolution" which has come into fashion as a convenient description of the system.[49] Yet the Kilbrandon Report used the expression to describe all existing arrangements for the conduct of government in Scotland, Wales and the English regions.[50]

The political weakness of administrative devolution is most evident when the majority of Scottish M.P.s and the majority in the House of Commons come from different parties (as they did between 1959 and 1964 and between 1970 and 1974).[51] Leaving aside the distorting effect of the electoral system, a Conservative Secretary of State's claim to be Scotland's Minister becomes rather transparent when his government persists with policies affecting Scottish domestic administration which would be rejected by Scotland's elected representatives. The short-lived scheme of museum charges provided a picquant example of the political absurdity that may arise, the Museums and Galleries Admission Charges Bill 1971 being introduced on Second Reading by the Lord Advocate because, it was said, of the special legal difficulties involved in legislating for the terms of bequests to Scottish museums and galleries to be overridden.[52] Similar problems in the same period arose in relation to the abolition of free milk for the under 11s, and council rent legislation; and the Conservatives would have had serious political difficulties in handling the oil construction-site planning applications in Scotland had there not been a General Election in February 1974.

Fifthly, the shortcomings of the political structure have accentuated the problem of maintaining a flow of Scottish legislation. With the development of the Scottish legislative committees at Westminster, shortage of House of Commons time is not in itself a reason for delays in Scottish legislation. More important factors have been the capacity of the Executive to prepare legislation (which has meant a large back-log of overdue statutory consolidation); on some topics, a lack of the necessary political and administrative will to legislate; a structural weakness in the Scottish political system whereby Scottish pressures for reform lose their impact before they are felt in London — and English pressures for reform lose their impact before they are felt in Scotland; and, above all, the fact that Scottish law-making remains part of a legislative process characterised (at least until February 1974) by executive dominance. The Scottish legislative committees have had to conform to the general pattern by which Parliament is managed. For this reason the proposal of the Conservative

100

Party's Constitutional Committee for a Scottish Assembly at Edinburgh to undertake certain stages of Scottish Bills passing through Westminster[53] would have made no appreciable difference.

The Scottish Legal System

Finally, the Union agreement of 1707 is now seen to be defective in that, while it guaranteed the future existence of the Scottish courts and the legal profession, it left the legal system with no legislature except the Westminster Parliament. Article 18 of the Treaty of Union provided for the laws in Scotland to be alterable by the Parliament of Great Britain —

"with this difference betwixt the laws concerning public right, policy and civil government, and those which concern private right; the laws which govern public right, policy, and civil government may be made the same throughout the whole United Kingdom; but that no alteration may be made in laws which concern private right except for the evident utility of the subjects within Scotland".

Recently a Banff fisherman has asked the Court of Session to declare that the European Communities Act 1972 would lead to a breach of this Article because of its eventual effect in opening Scottish inshore fishing to fishermen from EEC countries[53a] In 1921, a Scottish judge held that certain legislation which had been challenged was "for the evident utility of the subjects within Scotland".[54] But it is not at all certain the Scottish courts today would be prepared to review legislation on this ground. In any event, a more teasing distinction than that drawn between matters of public right and private right could hardly be devised for most modern legislation. Possibly in earlier times a legal system could survive without frequent legislative activity. But that is not the case today. While legislative policies of first importance to a determined Government will pass into law despite the inconvenience or embarrassment resulting from the political structure, on matters of secondary importance which attract opposition from Scottish circles, the probable outcome is that legislative reform is delayed. The development of the Scottish legislative committees and the work of the Scottish Law Commission since 1965 have not overcome this structural weakness. There is now a wide range of technical procedures for enabling Westminster to legislate more or less simultaneously for two distinct legal systems[55] but, as with other legislative decisions of the Executive, the choice of procedure in a particular case may be dictated by short-term political considerations.[56]

It is therefore not difficult to understand why feelings of instability and insecurity are often associated with the Scottish legal system. In fact, because of the lack of an indigenous legislature, the judiciary and the legal profession have a degree of autonomy which contrasts sharply with the complete absence of legislative autonomy and the restricted scope for administrative autonomy. The paucity of Scottish lawyers at Westminster is symptomatic of a distortion in the relationship of legislature, executive and judiciary,[57] and must reduce the effectiveness of Parliamentary scrutiny of Bills below even the general standard prevailing for British legislation. Another symptom of disorder is the fact that responsibility for the machinery of justice in Scotland has been shared rather uncertainly between the Secretary of State and the Lord Advocate, whose department falls outside the Scottish Office.[58] In 1972 a re-allocation of these functions[59] and the creation of the Scottish Courts Administration has made some improvement but may not be a final solution. The procedure for the appointment of judges still bears strong marks of the 18th century, even though we may have seen the last of the unhappy convention by which the Lord Advocate promoted himself whenever a vacancy occured in the two senior posts of Lord President and Lord Justice Clerk.[60]

The Kilbrandon Report

Eight of the thirteen members of the Commission on the Constitution recommended legislative devolution for Scotland, the most advanced scheme of devolution which the Commission were prepared to consider. Under this scheme, power would be vested in a Scottish Assembly to determine policy on a fairly wide range of subjects, to enact legislation to give effect to that policy and to provide the administrative machinery for its execution.[61] Professor Daintith has pointed out above that the fundamental disagreement over Scotland on the Commission lay between the majority of eight recommending legislative devolution, and the minority of four who rejected the creation of special constitutional arrangements for Scotland and Wales alone. The advantages of legislative devolution would be primarily to subject Scottish administration to a new level of political leadership and a new measure of democratic accountability; to introduce new legislative procedures within the developed areas of government; to provide a forum for Scottish political opinion; and to enable Scottish organs to influence more directly environmental, industrial and economic development. In the remainder of this paper, it is proposed to discuss a number of issues relevant to these majority recommendations.

A.   While it is natural to consider as a basis for devolution the work at present done by the Scottish Office, hitherto the Scottish Office has been part of a single system of government which in all its operations has assumed political and administrative unity.[62] What is proposed is a fundamental difference of structure and control. For example, in relation to the police, the Kilbrandon Report apparently considered that the central government must retain responsibility for the preservation of law and order.[63] In Scotland, the Secretary of State has complete responsibility for the police, which is administered under Scottish legislation: would the U.K. government wish to devolve this responsibility upon a Scottish government? The working of any scheme of legislative devolution would require a new set of working relationships to be developed across the border between British and Scottish administrators and politicians. Hitherto, the existence of separate legislation regarding the police or education or the National Health Service has indicated neither the degree of uniformity nor the permissible degree of diversity. Thus the present allocation of functions to the Scottish Office may not be a reliable guide to the functions which the U.K. government might be willing to devolve to a subordinate government. Devolution of areas like education, in which there is a strong Scottish tradition supported by the teaching profession, would probably be easier than of areas like the National Health Service (where the relevant professional organisations would be likely to press for uniformity on matters affecting them) or energy, in which there is a national strategic interest and in which there is no long tradition of Scottish administration. An unknown factor is the future development of the Scottish political system and its relationship to British politics generally.

B.   Again and again the Kilbrandon Report stressed the need to maintain the essential political and economic unity of the U.K. Thus, "we believe that the essential political and economic unity of the U.K. should be preserved. Subject to that, diversity should be recognised".[64] What specific content does the Report give to the concept of essential political and economic unity? Or is it merely a conveniently vague formula for indicating that ultimately the U.K. Parliament and Government must have power to take the steps which they think necessary in the interests of the U.K.? Presumably, by analogy with the Luxemburg Agreement within EEC, only the State itself is capable of deciding what are its vital national interests. Presumably too, the Kilbrandon Report did not intend the concept to be invoked as a means of blocking any change in the existing system.

The Report gives both helpful and unhelpful clues about this concept. Early in the Report are set out the main characteristics of the existing Union: (1) a common loyalty to the Crown; (2) a common citizenship; (3) representation of all citizens within the U.K. Parliament, which has supreme law-making authority; (4) in economic and financial matters, a single currency and banking system; and complete freedom of movement for trade, labour and capital within the U.K; and (5) when allowance has been made for the distinct legal systems within the U.K, a common subjection of all citizens to the same law.[65] For the future, the principle of economic and political unity is held to require: (1) that the U.K. Parliament should retain its legislative sovereignty; (2) that the U.K. Government and Parliament must retain such financial and economic powers as are necessary to maintain a stable economy; (3) that the different parts of the U.K. must maintain reasonable equality in the standards of public services (since an excessive divergence in these standards would undermine political and economic unity); and (4) that the U.K. Government must minimise regional disparities in economic conditions.[66] But the concept of unity does not exclude the devolution of some freedom to make public expenditure decisions, does not require absolute uniformity in the standards of public services, and does not exclude the devolution of some limited powers of taxation. The Report considers that economic and political unity does *not* require a uniform structure of government throughout the U.K. (i.e. Scottish voters may elect two Parliaments while English voters elect only one) and does *not* require any formal constitutional means for protecting basic human rights though it does require equality of basic democratic rights (e.g. women in Scotland under the age of 30 could not be excluded from voting for a Scottish assembly).

So far as legislative devolution is concerned, economic and political unity would be safeguarded in three ways: (1) by maintaining the sovereignty of the U.K. Parliament, (2) by the proposal to finance the devolved services on the expenditure basis and not the revenue basis, and (3) by the proposed power of disallowance for devolved legislation. The power of disallowance or veto would be necessary, says the Report, (a) to ensure compliance with international obligations, (b) to safeguard "some other essential British interest" and (c) "to prevent adoption of policies considered to be inconsistent with the maintenance of the essential political and economic unity of the U.K."[67]

As to (a), it might be commented that the effect of section 2(a) of the European Communities Act 1972 is presumably to make disallowance redundant where the international obligations arise under Community treaties — since these obligations would override any inconsistent legislation within the U.K. As for (b) and (c), vagueness of this high order suggests that the extent of devolution is essentially to be a matter for day-to-day political decision.[68] But unless clear guidelines are developed for the safeguarded interests, even the scheme of legislative devolution could turn out in practice to be little different from executive devolution, or, for that matter, from the pre-Kilbrandon era. If such reserve powers are to be maintained in the devolved fields, it is probable that, since nothing of great import will turn on the statutory terms of devolution, these can be made broad enough to make judicial review of devolved action virtually a non-starter, while allowing full scope for political and administrative interpretation.

C. It follows necessarily from the "essential political unity" approach that the Kilbrandon Report eschews the use of legal safeguards. In a federal system, the constitution itself specifies the matters on which it is essential for political and economic unity to be maintained. The Report not merely excludes federalism from consideration, it also dismisses (after a few paragraphs of superficial and poorly argued discussion, which fails even to refer to U.K. obligations under the European Convention on Human Rights) protection by a Bill of Rights against legislative or executive abuse by the devolved organs of government. The Report also fails to grasp the significance of administrative law to a devolved system of government despite the forceful arguments made by Professor Mitchell.[69] The opportunity for an advance in each of these fields of public law seems to have been rejected because of the implications of such an advance for the whole system of government in the U.K.

105

D.   One of the major tasks of British central government in matters of domestic administration is not to administer the services directly but to supervise local authorities who actually provide the services. This supervision takes many forms, differing in methods, intensity, purpose and so on. Professor Griffith has shown how different departments of central government interpret their role of supervision differently.[70] In Scotland, local authorities have been supervised by the various departments of the Scottish Office. In recent years, the control of expenditure by local authorities has become an important economic weapon for central government. Will the U.K. government be persuaded to part with its direct relationship with local government? And will citizens affected by local decisions, and local authorities themselves, be disposed to accept that these powers of supervision should be exercised finally at an intermediate level? If the Scottish and U.K. governments differ politically, there will be an added tendency to appeal upwards to the most favourable level. Theoretically devolution of the supervision of local authorities should prevent too many local political issues going to the centre and thus ease the burden at Westminster. What would happen in practice? The problem of enforcing the law against recalcitrant local authorities would be aggravated if they had the political support of the Scottish Assembly on a matter which the U.K. Government insisted was a matter of essential political unity.

E.   The issue of oil development would pose difficult questions even for a well-established scheme of devolution. In this area too, the U.K. Government would hardly wish to relinquish the present powers of the Secretary of State for Scotland to a Scottish government. It is one thing to permit a Secretary of State within the U.K. Cabinet to make decisions on oil-related planning applications. It is quite another to devolve the power to a Scottish government. Legislatively, it would be perfectly possible for oil-related applications to be excluded from the general devolution of town planning functions. A possible expedient that might be more acceptable politically would be the creation of a new specialised agency which might have some kind of joint responsibility both to the U.K. Parliament and the Scottish Assembly, but at which level would the strategic decisions on development and the environment be made?

F.   The Kilbrandon Commission could hardly have foreseen the strategic importance and political sensitivity that oil would assume but were in a position to consider fully the scope for devo-

lution in the economic and industrial field. The Report's acceptance of the official view that economic and industrial
development is a British responsibility which should not be
devolved has been challenged very strongly by those who see the
main advantage in devolution as being the chance of new industrial initiatives originating in the region concerned. Thus an
economist has regretted that the Kilbrandon Report did not inves-
tigate the implications of devolving trade, industry and employment functions with any rigour.[71] A report published by the
Scottish Council Research Institute[72] has argued that present
arrangements for Scottish economic policy are a "manifest fiction", since nominal responsibility for economic coordination
rests with the Scottish Office but effective powers lie with British
departments. Moreover, since control over the physical pattern of
development rests with the Scottish Office, "there is no one body
which can evolve a co-ordinated development strategy which is
based on a coherent synthesis of economic and physical considerations".[73] The report comments that legislative devolution to Scotland should include trade, industry, employment and the
nationalised industries and also prices and incomes legislation
and industrial relations. In company with the authors of the
Memorandum of Dissent to the Kilbrandon Report and the
House of Commons Committee on Expenditure, the report is
sceptical of the success of current methods of central management of the economy. It recommends "an end to persuasion and
the start of negotiation"[74] so that "the overall management of the
Scottish economy would become part of a system of formalised
bargaining, rather than being centrally directed".[75] This would
not threaten the economic and political unity of the U.K., it is
argued, for any scheme of devolution means that unity is no
longer absolute: the balance between devolution and unity "cannot be justified by any abstract principles alone and it will not
necessarily remain constant".[76] This makes good sense, although
in places the report verges on the fanciful (for example, in dealing with Scotland's relations with EEC, the U.K. government is
expected to become "an increasingly redundant intermediary
between a Scottish government and the EEC"[77]). But there is a
strong argument that the Kilbrandon Report failed to grasp the
economic and industrial nettle firmly enough to make proposals
of relevance to Scotland's economic situation.

G. It is very doubtful whether the Exchequer Board proposed
by Kilbrandon could function as it is described. Independent of

both the U.K. Government and the devolved governments, the Board members would be expected to perform their task "with moderation and commonsense".[78] For the Board to be other than a nonentity or a messenger-boy, greater constitutional protection would need to be given to it than the Kilbrandon Report suggests. In fact, it would be making important political decisions, and it would be better to look for a financial structure which would admit this.

H. Finally, although much still remains to be settled, and most of the important details will not be known until a Bill has been published, the Labour Government have given an undertaking that during the 1970s an elected Scottish Assembly will be created which will exercise some legislative powers and have the functions of calling some branches of Scottish administration to account. It would be a surprising departure from British constitutional development if the venture were not to be very strictly controlled by a variety of formal and informal means. Professor Bénoit, while demonstrating that there is a continuum between the slightest measure of decentralisation and the most extreme form of federalism, has suggested that not all points on the continuum are viable, in particular the solution called "provincialism". Bénoit describes "provincialism" as giving to a community legislative powers that do not include competence in matters concerning its own organisation. History teaches us, says Bénoit, that this solution has been adopted when a local population was wanting more than mere decentralisation, but when the central authorities were not willing to move so far as authentic federalism. "This solution appears inherently unstable: it is either too much or too little."[79]

Although the lessons of history may be harder to master than this judgment would suggest, the dangers of provincialism, impotence and instability lie ahead. The Kilbrandon Report considered that the Scottish Office and Welsh Office system works in Scotland and Wales "because they are regarded as special cases, singled out for exceptional treatment".[80] Probably the system was prevented from working as well as it might have done by many of the constraints of British politics and administration. There is nothing in the current state of discussion of devolution in Britain to suggest that there will be a general re-appraisal of these constraints or that there will be other constitutional gains for the U.K. as a whole or for England in particular.[81] This lack is bound to restrict the success of devolution to Scotland. In the future as in the past, special and general cases alike will have to flower in the same constitutional climate.

NOTES

[In these notes, except where otherwise indicated, "Report" means the Report of the Royal Commission on the Constitution, Volume I, 1973, Cmnd. 5460. "Dissent" means the Memorandum of Dissent, Royal Commission on the Constitution, Volume II, Cmnd. 5460-I. "Commission" means Royal Commission on the Constitution.]

1. R.G.S. Brown, The Administrative Process in Britain, 1971, p.214. See in particular Brown's criticism of the new Department of Health and Social Security, pp. 207-214.
2. R. v Greater Birmingham Appeal Tribunal, ex parte Simper (1973) 2 All E.R. 461.
3. Report of the Tribunal of Inquiry (1971-72) H.C. 133, H.L. 80.
4. White Paper, "The Reorganisation of Central Government", 1970, Cmnd. 4506.
5. Cmnd. 4506, para. 10.
6. R.G.S. Brown, op. cit.
7. Report, para. 203.
8. See the account in A.H. Hanson and M. Walles, Governing Britain, 1970, chap. 10.
9. Report of Royal Commission on Local Government in England, 1969, Cmnd. 4040, chap. 10; on Local Government in Scotland, 1969, Cmnd. 4150, paras. 683-686.
10. Royal Commission on Scottish Affairs, Minutes of Evidence, Day 8, p. 31.
11. Commission. Minutes of Evidence II (Scotland) p. 8.
12. E.g. Vedel, Droit Administratif, 5th edn. 1973, pp. 639-40 and Waline, Droit Administratif, 9th edn. 1963, pp. 302-305.
13. Waline, op.cit., p. 306. However, J.P. Bénoit, Le Droit Administratif Français, 1968, argues that to apply 'décentralisation' to local government is both a historical and an analytical error.
14. But see Hanson and Walles, op. cit., chap. 10, p. 210, where 'deconcentration' is used to describe 'the purely bureaucratic phenomenon'.

15. Report of the Committee on Scottish Administration, 1937, Cmd. 5563, para. 42.

16. Fesler, "Centralisation and Decentralisation", International Encylopedia of the Social Sciences, 1968, p. 371.

17. Ferguson, Scotland, 1689 to the Present, 1968, p. 133. And see P.W.J. Riley, The English Ministers and Scotland 1707-27, 1964, p. 96.

18. For accounts of the administrative history since 1707 see Milne, The Scottish Office, 1957, chap. 2; Hanham, Scottish Nationalism, 1969 chap. 3, and "The development of the Scottish Office" in Wolfe (Ed.) Government and Nationalism in Scotland, 1969; Kellas, Modern Scotland: The Nation since 1870, 1968, chap. 7, and The Scottish Political System, 1973, chaps. 2 and 3; and Ferguson, op. cit.

19. See the proposed Scottish Development Agency promised by the Government in Cmnd. 5732 (September 1974) para. 34, details of which were made known on 31 January 1975.

20. Report of the Committee on Scottish Administration, 1937, Cmd. 5563, para. 18.

21. Handbook on Scottish Administration, H.M.S.O. 1967, page 3.

22. Hanham, "The Development of the Scottish Office", op. cit., at p. 63.

23. For details of the first four departments, see Commission, Written Evidence, 2 and for the Economic Planning Department, see Report, para. 98.

24. Report of the Committee on Scottish Administration, para. 37.

25. See the Treasury Memorandum of June 1946 on Departmental Organisation, printed in Appendix VII of the Report of the Royal Commission on Scottish Affairs, 1954, Cmd. 9212; and paras. 253-261 of this Report.

26. Report of the Royal Commission on Scottish Affairs, para. 13.

27. Op. cit., para. 116.

28. See the evidence of Bridges and Haddow quoted in para. 5 above.

29. Milne, op. cit., p. 21.

30. Report, para. 98.

31. Commission, Minutes of Evidence, II, pp. 8 and 12; Report, para. 1049.

32. Report, para. 1022.

33. "Devolution within the U.K.: Some Alternatives for Discussion", 1974, H.M.S.O. But on 20 December 1974, the Prime Minister announced that responsibility for selective regional assistance to industry was to be transferred to the Secretary of State for Scotland with effect from July 1975 (H.C. Deb. W.A. Col. 712)

34. J.G. Kellas, The Scottish Political System, pp. 54-55.

35. For the complexities of agriculture, see J.D.B. Mitchell "Government and

Public Law in Scotland", in Andrews (Ed.) Welsh Studies in Public Law, p.76.

36. Kellas, op.cit., p.59.

37. Kellas, op.cit., p.66.

38. Mitchell, op.cit., p.76

39. Mitchell, op.cit., pp. 76-83 and see also Commission, written evidence, Vol. 9, p. 137.

40. Cf. Kellas, op.cit., p.47.

41. Commission, Minutes of Evidence II, p. 10.

42. Scottish Council Research Institute Report, "Economic Development and Devolution", p. 21.

43. Both the Scottish Economic Planning Council and the Highlands and Islands Development Board have been criticised for excessive secrecy. The deliberations of the former are said to be confidential because it is giving advice to the Secretary of State; on the latter, see H.McN. Henderson, "The Highlands and Islands Development Board" in Friedmann and Garner (Eds.), Government Enterprise, p. 101.

44. For a fuller argument to this effect, see Commission, Written Evidence, 5, pp. 50-52.

45. Para. 92 of the Report has to be read alongside the oral evidence on this point: Commission, Minutes of Evidence II, pp. 24-28.

46. Commission, Written Evidence, 2, p. 5.

47. Commission, Minutes of Evidence, II, p. 19.

48. Commission, Minutes of Evidence, II, p. 12.

49. "Administrative devolution" was not used by the Gilmour Committee in 1937 nor by Milne in The Scottish Office in 1957. It was used in Parliament to explain the limited terms of reference of the Balfour Commission (Cmd. 9212, p. 10), but not in the Balfour Report itself. But both Mackintosh, in The Devolution of Power, 1968, pp. 110-133 and the Report of the Scottish Constitutional Committee of the Conservative Party, Scotland's Government, 1970, give prominence to the expression.

50. Report, chap. 21, para. 978.

51. Giving evidence in 1969, Sir Douglas Haddow professed not to know whether this had ever happened: Commission, Minutes of Evidence II, p. 20.

52. House of Commons, Hansard, 25 January 1972, cols. 1206-1221.

53. See the Report of the Committee, Scotland's Government, 1970, chap. 6.

53a. Scotsman, 12-14 February 1975

54. Laughland v. Wansborough Paper Co. Ltd. 1921 (1) S.L.T. 341.

55. See e.g. Commission, Written Evidence, 5, Memoranda by the Lord Advocate's Department, pp. 25-27, and the Scottish Law Commission, pp. 28-31.

56. Commission, Written Evidence, 5, Memorandum by the Lord Advocate's Department, pp. 25-27, and Minutes of Evidence II, pp. 16-17.

57. Cf. Commission, Written Evidence, 5, Memorandum by the Faculty of Advocates, p. 8.

58. Commission, Written Evidence, 5, Supplementary memorandum by the Lord Advocate's Department, pp. 21-25.

59. H.C. Hansard, 21 December 1972, W.A.col. 455.

60. The present holders of the two senior judicial posts, Lord Emslie and Lord Wheatley, were already serving as judges before they were promoted. But the last act of Mr. Norman Wylie as Lord Advocate, before the general election in February 1974, was to recommend his own name for appointment to the Court of Session, a vacancy having been conveniently retained for the purpose.

61. Report, para. 734.

62. See the note of warning sounded on the Report, para. 708.

63. Report, Appendix D, para. 115. But cf. para. 1132 of the Report which suggests that police would be transferred.

64. Report, para. 1104.

65. Report, paras. 53-59.

66. Report, para. 583.

67. Report, para. 765.

68. Cf. Report, paras. 25, 582.

69. Commission, Written Evidence, 9, pp. 131-144.

70. J.A.G. Griffith, Central Departments and Local Authorities, 1966.

71. J.R. Fern, "The Benefits of coherent development strategy" in The Scotsman, 26 June 1974. Fern's criticism could also be applied to other sections of Appendix D to the Report, which purports to examine the scope for devolution of departmental functions. How much of this was based uncritically upon departmental attitudes?

72. "Economic Development and Devolution", June 1974, by C.R. Dunn and S.I. Chorley.

73. Op. cit., p. 21.

74. Op. cit., p. 21.

75. Op. cit., p. 24.

76. Op. cit., p. 28.

77. Op. cit., p. 30.

78. Report, p.206.

79. F-P. Bénoit, Le Droit Administratif Français, 1968, p. 134, (translated).

80. Report, para. 1030.

81. Cf. Dissent, para. 119.

VII RECENT DEVELOPMENTS IN DEVOLUTION IN BELGIUM.

K. Rimanque *

In this paper , I shall try briefly to sketch some recent developments in Belguim connected with the general problem of devolution of government. Most problems of re-organisation of the institutional machinery of the state are connected with the main political issue of the moment which is the pacification of the antagonism between the two principal cultural communities. Not only in the cultural sphere are there differences between the north, the south and the capital district. Economic, social and demographic problems are quite different, and politically there is a growing Flemish, Walloon and capital feeling among the population, or at least among the politicians. The unitary state is outstripped by the actual political situation: this is not a personal opinion, but it is a statement of a former prime minister, Viscount G. Eyskens.

A. *Planning and economic decentralization*

Planning and economic decentralization are introduced at the same time as the constitutional recognition of the cultural autonomy of the communities: they are provided by an act of 15 July 1970. In general there was more interest in cultural autonomy among the Flemish population amd more interest in economic self-determination among the Walloon public opinion.

The keystone of the economic planning is the five-year plan, which is prepared by the national planning Bureau which has three dimensions: a general, a sectorial and a regional direction. After many consultations with other authorities the plan has to be approved by the Houses of Parliament. The plan is binding upon public authorities and has the value of a contractual obliga-

* Professor of Constitutional Law, University of Antwerp.

tion for the state supported enterprises. For other enterprises it has an indicative value only.

From the point of devolution economic decentralization is more important. The law established three regional economic Councils: for Flanders, for Wallonia and for the province of Brabant. But the Flemish districts of this province fall also within the jurisdiction of the Flemish Council and the French districts within the jurisdiction of the Walloon Council, because these districts are Flemish or Walloon territory.

These Councils are composed of five kinds of members: members of Parliament; members of the provincial Councils; representatives of organisations of industry, large non-industrial enterprises, shopkeepers and agriculture; representatives of trade unions and economic experts. The politicians have an equal number of seats as so-called social partners. The composition of the Council for Brabant is rather complicated: there must be equality between members of the capital district and of the rest of the province; the Council for Flanders and the Council for Wallonia have a right to elect the latter group of members — parity between Dutch and French-speaking members is a legal obligation.

The regional economic Councils are consultative bodies. They study the economic problems of their region, they give advice about the appointment of public servants in the regional dimension of the planning Bureau, about the areas of the regional development corporations, about the distribution of the budget for regional economic expansion and their employment for public and social equipment. They also have advisory competence about drafts of acts and regulations in connection with regional development. They have to adopt the regional economic plan and to co-ordinate the activities of regional development corporations.

The regional development corporations are the executive branches of the regional Councils. In principle the initiative for their foundation has to be taken by the provincial Councils, on the advice of the regional economic Council, but the King in Council decides about their areas. A corporation can be competent for one or several provinces. The corporations study and plan the promotion of the economic development of their areas, they make a list of the needs of their region and co-operate with the planning Bureau in the conception and execution of the Plan. In this respect, they have a general competence of proposition, stimulation and co-ordination with regard to the promotion of economic activities, town and country planning, social equipment and regional structures. They can expropriate, sell land and do all other acts, which according to the Plan may encourage private and public investment. If a private company should fail, a regional development corporation can, with the technical and financial co-operation of the National Investment Corporation take the initiative for industrial projects. To summarize, regional development corporations can do all acts and things for the economic promotion of their area under the supervision of the regional economic Council and the financial control of the government.

It is possible that these institutions for regional economic development will be replaced, when a more global structure of regional organization is worked out in execution of the new constitutional provision about regionalism.

B. *Political regionalism in Belgium.*

The present legislature has to find a solution to the problem of the introduction of regional institutions in Belgium. In 1970 a new provision was introduced into the constitution to that end. It almost happened by accident; indeed, political regionalism was not included in the preliminary programme for constitutional amendment during previous legislatures. The principle of regionalism was agreed during informal meetings of the leaders of all political parties. The text of the constitutional provision (see annexe A) is short and general: almost everything remains possible. According to some experts, even federal institutions could be legally acceptable under this section of the constitution. But the vagueness of section 107 quater makes it very difficult to find the necessary special majority in Parliament for a specific plan for the execution of this constitutional provision. At the moment, there is no such solution.

On the initiative of the present government, both Houses of Parliament have adopted a preparatory act, with a common majority, which vests advisory competences in three regional groups of senators on particular subjects and establishes three special committees of ministers and junior ministers for regional affairs. It is agreed that the National Parliament can adopt acts, applicable only in a particular region, just as the Parliament of Westminster can legislate for England and Wales or for Scotland.

117

This is of course not the execution of the regional provision of the constitution. In the meantime, the government hopes that it will become possible to obtain some experience about the problems of regional organization.

The constitution says there are three regions in Belgium: the Flemish & Walloon regions and the region of Brussels. Without constitutional amendment no more regions can be established. The boundaries of the regions are to be fixed by law. This is a very delicate political problem, especially in respect to the area of the region of Brussels. It is obvious that the sphere of social and economic influence of the capital reaches further than the actual bilingual linguistic region. But it unlikely that Flemish public opinion accepts a larger area for Brussels. And as a result, this point of view gives a good reason for a number of politicians from Brussels (members of the *Front des Francophones* in particular) to oppose existing plans for regional organization. But they have to remember that the operation aims at political regions, and not at economic spheres of influence.

Regional institutions must be composed of elected members. The question is, whether to organise new and specific elections or to form the regional Councils from existing political bodies, as in the case of the Cultural Councils. In the second hypothesis, there are many possibilities: the members of both Houses of Parliament, the members of the House of Representatives or of the Senate only, all or some members of the provincial Councils, a mixture of members of Parliament and provincial councillors and for the region of Brussels even councillors of the capital district (*conseil d'agglomeration*). In my opinion, in the long run, the best thing to do is, through new constitutional amendment, to abolish one of the two Houses of Parliament and to organize specific regional elections for a pool of regional councillors, divided into two councils for cultural affairs, and into three councils for regional affairs.

The constitution does not exculde the establishment of a regional executive college or regional government. But governments since 1970 have not been attracted by that idea. They prefer regional ministers and junior ministers within central government. They claim the necessity of co-ordination and the priority of national policy.

The regional institutions have, under the actual constitution, no tax competence. Probably there will be a regional appropriation distributed among the three regions, according to the following formula: $^1/_3$ according to area, $^1/_3$ according to the population, $^1/_3$ according to the amount of the income tax yield of natural persons.

Ratione materiae, the constitution authorizes the delegation of almost any competence to the regional authorities, with the exception of the regulation of the use of languages and all matters within the competence of the Cultural Councils. Of course nobody thinks of the regionalization of civil or penal code provisions, the army, monetary policy, etc. ... At the moment, all schemes are made by reference to a list of competences suggested by the conference of the leaders of the political parties in 1969. This list includes:

- Urbanism, town and country planning, real estate policy;
- regional policy in connection with economic expansion and employment;
- some aspects of industrial legislation and energy policy;
- housing;
- family and demographic policy;
- sanitary and public health policy;
- professional training and occupational resettlement;
- tourism;
- the fishing industry, hunting and forest administration.

The place of regional regulation in the legal hierarchy is not clearly provided for in the constitution. On purpose the constitution speaks of *régler*, a very general legal term in Belgium. As in the case of decrees of the Cultural Councils, it is not excluded that with special delegation regional regulations could change or abolish legal provisions. According to the preparatory works of the constitutional provision, regional regulations will enjoy the same status as royal decrees.

C. *Federations of Municipalities and Urban Districts.*

Belgium has always been a decentralized state: provinces and municipalities are autonomous political bodies, with their own spheres of competence, elected councils and executive authorities and act under the supervision of the central authorities. In particular the municipal autonomy of the more than 2,000 communes has always been one of the major aspects of political life in Belgium. But in the contemporary situation, small municipalities do not have the necessary financial resources nor the qualified civil servants to establish and to manage all the kinds of social and cultural services, which are expected from these authorities. On the other hand, around the major cities the municipalities have grown and form one agglomeration with the central city. Co-operation between the city and the surrounding communes is a necessity for the good management and administration of the whole urban district.

As a result of these political developments a constitutional law of 1970 introduced a new concept in local government: the establishment of federations of municipalities and urban districts. The legislature can organize and establish such federations and districts, having regard to the constitutional principles on local government (section 108 bis of the constitution). The urban district of Brussels is subject to special provisions, because of the tensions between the two major cultural communities (section 108 ter; annexe B). An act of Parliament of 26 July 1971 provides the general scheme for the organization of these federations and districts and has established the capital district and five federations of (Flemish) municipalities around Brussels. But there is no constitutional obligation to establish other federations or urban districts and, so far as I can see, it is not likely that other such municipal superstructures will be established in the near future.

In fact it is more likely that the problem of the too small municipalities will be solved by means of unification of adjacent municipalities. In 1962 more than two thirds of the municipalities numbered less then 2,000 inhabitants. On the other hand many suburban communities have too strong a political identity (many of their Mayors and Aldermen are members of Parliament) to be easily united with the city. In addition, it would be wrong to underestimate the political consequences of the unification of existing municipalities: Mayors and Aldermen have to disappear: there is the possibility of new perhaps unwanted political majorities, etc.

The organization of Federations of municipalities and Urban Districts is similar to that of provinces and municipalities. The inhabitants elect a council (the number of the councillors depends on the number of inhabitants). The councillors elect the Court. Unlike the Court of Mayor and Aldermen in the municipality the Court is not only composed of members of the political majority in the Council: in this case every political party elects Aldermen in proportion to its number of seats in the Council. The Mayor is elected by the majority of votes in the Council. His election has to be sanctioned by the King. Federations and Urban

Districts have their own administration.

These municipal superstructures take over many competences of the communes:
- competences in connection with town and country planning;
- building and letting permits;
- collection and disposal of refuse;
- water distribution;
- local transportation of persons;
- protection of the environment;
- fire brigades;
- urgent medical assistance.

The federations and urban districts may also exercise other municipal competences, at the request of at least half the number of the municipalities of the federation, on condition that they represent two thirds of the inhabitants. These additional and facultative competences are:
- management of roads;
- airports;
- fixing of the places for open markets;
- slaughter houses;
- public parking;
- promotion of tourism and tourist-information;
- camping and caravanning;
- cremation and cemeteries;
- establishment ot technical services for the municipalities.

According to the constitution (sections 110 and 113) the federations have a tax competence; they can levy taxes by means of surcharges on provincial real estate, income and traffic taxes, with royal assent. As in the case of the municipalities, there is an administrative supervision on the acts and decisions of the Federations and Urban Districts. In some cases authorization or approval of the higher authority is necessary; all regulations or decisions which are illegal or are contrary to the general interest can be set aside. The government (especially the Minister of the Interior) supervises the urban districts, and the executive Court of the provincial Councils supervise the Federations of municipalities.

Annexe A.

Baudouin, etc.

Les Chambres ont adopté dans les conditions prescrites par l'article 131 de la Constitution, et Nous sanctionnons ce qui suit:

Article unique. Il est inséré dans la Constitution au Titre III, sous un Chapitre IIIter — "Des institutions régionales" — un article 107quater, libellé comme suit:

"Article 107 quater. La Belgique comprend trois regions: la région wallonne, la région flamande et la région bruxelloise.

"La loi attribue aux organes régionaux qu'elle crée et qui sont composés de mandataires élus, la competence de régler les matières qu'elle détermine, à l'exception de celles visées aux articles 23 et 59bis, dans le ressort et selon le mode qu'elle établit.

"Cette loi doit être adoptée à la majorité des suffrages dans chaque groupe linguistique de chacune des Chambres, à la condition que la majorité des membres de chaque groupe se trouve réunie et pour autant que le total des votes positifs émis dans les deux groupes linguistiques atteigne les deux tiers des suffrages exprimés."

Promulguons, etc.

Annexe B.

Baudouin, etc.

Les Chambres ont adopté dans les conditions prescrites par l'article 131 de la Constitution, et Nous sanctionnons ce qui suit:

Article unique. La Constitution est complétée par un article 108bis libellé comme suit:

"Art. 108bis § 1. La loi crée des agglomérations et des fédérations de communes. Elle détermine leur organisation et leur competence en consacrant l'application des principes énoncés a l'article 108.

"Il y a pour chaque agglomération et pour chaque fédération un conseil et un collège exécutif.

"Le président du collège exécutif est élu par le conseil, en son sein; son élection est ratifiée par le Roi; la loi règle son statut.

"Les articles 107 et 129 s'appliquent aux arrêtes et règlements des agglomérations et des fédérations de communes.

"Les limites des agglomérations et des fédérations de communes ne peuvent être changées ou rectifiées qu'en vertu d'une loi.

"§2. La loi crée l'organe au sein duquel chaque agglomération

122

et les fédérations de communes les plus proches se concertent aux conditions et selon le mode qu'elle fixe, pour l'examen de problèmes communs de caractère technique qui relèvent de leur compétence respective.

"§3. Plusieurs fédérations de communes peuvent s'entendre ou s'associer entre elles ou avec une ou plusieurs agglomérations dans les conditions et suivant le mode à déterminer par la loi pour régler et gérer en commun des objets qui relèvent de leur competence. Il n'est pas permis a leurs conseils de délibérer en commun."

Baudouin, etc.

Les Chambres ont adopté dans les conditions prescrites par l'article 131 de la Constitution, et Nous sanctionnons ce qui suit:

Article unique, La Constitution est complétée par un article 108ter, libellé comme suit:

"Article 108ter. § a. L'article 108bis s'applique à l'agglomération à laquelle appartient la capitale du Royaume sous réserve de ce qui est prévu ci-après.

§ 2. Pour les cas déterminés dans la Constitution et dans la loi, les membres du conseil de l'agglomération sont répartis en un groupe linguistique français et un groupe linguistique néerlandais de la manière fixée par la loi.

"Le collège exécutif est composé d'un nombre impair de membres. Le président excepté, il compte autant de membres du groupe linguistique français que du groupe linguistique néerlandais.

"§ 3. Sauf pour les budgets, une motion motivée, signée par les trois quarts au moins des membres d'un groupe linguistique du conseil de l'agglomération, et introduite avant le vote final en séance publique, peut déclarer que les dispositions qu'elle désigne dans un projet ou une proposition, de règlement ou d'arrêté du conseil d'agglomération peuvent porter gravement atteinte aux relations entre les communautés.

"Dans ce cas la procédure au sein du conseil d'agglomération est suspendue et la motion est renvoyée au collège exécutif qui, dans les trente jours émet son avis motivé à ce sujet et amende le projet ou la proposition s'il échet.

"La tutelle relative au règlement ou à l'arrêté pris après cette procédure, est exercée par le Roi sur proposition du Conseil des Ministres.

"Cette procédure ne peut être appliquée qu'une fois par les membres d'un groupe linguistique concernant un même projet ou une même proposition.

"§4. Dans l'agglomération, il existe une commission française de la culture et une commission néerlandaise de la culture, qui sont composées d'un même nombre de membres élus respectivement par le groupe linguistique français et par le groupe linguistique néerlandais du conseil d'agglomération.

"Elles ont, chacune pour la communauté culturelle, les mêmes compétences que les autres pouvoirs organisateurs:

1⁰ en matière préscolaire, postscolaire et culturelle:

2⁰ en matière d'enseignement.

"§5. La commission française et la commission néerlandaise de la culture constituent ensemble les Commissions réunies. Les décisions des Commissions réunies ne sont adoptées que si elles obtiennent dans chaque commission la majorité des voix émises.

Les Commissions réunies sont competentes pour les matières prévues au § 4 qui sont d'intérêt commun et pour la promotion de la mission nationale et internationale de l'agglomération.

"§ 6. Les commissions visées aux §§ 4 et 5 remplissent également les missions dont elles sont chargées par le pouvoir legislatif, les conseils culturels ou le gouvernement.

"La loi règle l'organisation et le fonctionnement de ces commissions."

Promulguons, etc.

VIII   DECENTRALIZATION IN FRANCE
J. de Forges*

The English word "devolution" will be translated in this article by the French word "decentralisation", which is in current use. For purposes of clarity it must be stated that this word "decentralisation" has two meanings: it conveys both the result of the division of jurisdiction to the advantage of local authorities (English "self government") and the action of conferring jurisdiction to local authorities (English "devolution").

I   *General system of division of jurisdiction in France*

1.   *France is not a federal, but a unitary state;* it is permitted, however, for public groups other than the state to independently govern their own affairs. This is the basic idea behind "decentralisation"; in this respect it is very close to the British "self government".

Within the state there exist three categories of public law bodies in France: "departments", "communes" and "public establishments". These are the three categories which profit from decentralisation. The departments and communes govern affairs of local interest, each at their own level; they correspond to what is termed "provincial decentralisation" (close to the British "local government"). The public establishments, which are extremely numerous and varied, normally embody public services and this is known as "technical decentralisation" or "decentralisation according to services" (examples of public establishments: the universities; the Chambers of Commerce; the French Television Broadcasting Corporation (ORTF); Institute of Oil Research and Activity; Electricité de France; Paris airport.)

* Professor of Law, University of Nancy.

2. Characteristics of decentralisation

Decentralised public groups have the following features:

a) They have their own affairs: it is recognised that local groups (departments and communes) are the expression of a community of interest among their inhabitants. Administrative law recognises this by qualifying these particular affairs as "local affairs"; this means that local groups do not have the right to intervene in those fields which are not encompassed in "local affairs". Here it must be stressed that it is the organs of state, i.e. the Parliament which determine the field of local affairs. Decentralisation is thus very different from federalism since by the nature of French law local jurisdiction has in effect no authority.

Corresponding to the concept of "local affairs", there exists, in the case of the public establishments the "principle of specialisation"; a public establishment is essentially created to run a selected service (e.g. the public service of higher education in the case of the universities) or to embody a group of people (e.g. the farmers in each department all form part of the "Departmental Chamber of Agriculture"); it may not interfere in any field which is outside its own "speciality".

b) It governs its own affairs; this is the most delicate point, and the most discussed. It is recognised that a system is only decentralised when the authority entrusted with running a public group is attached to it very closely on a personal level. Thus, the communes are run by municipal councils and a mayor elected from among the inhabitants; and the departments are administered by a "General Council" elected by their inhabitants. But it is not certain that the election system is necessary: the head of the local administration could be nominated by the state from *among* the inhabitants of the local group in question. This point of view is becoming more and more redundant, however: the notion of democracy seems to imply a system of election.

Self government of the public establishments is more difficult to implement: in certain cases, the governing bodies are elected (e.g. Councils and Presidents in the universities), but very often they are nominated by the state, particularly in the case of establishments engaged in industrial ectivity; in this case, moreover, the President or the Director is aided by an administrative council which almost always includes members of the personnel and "customers" of the establishment.

c) It is under the trusteeship of the state: this is the most original, but also the most difficult aspect of decentralisation to explain. The trustee method of supervision is a very particular type of control which is much less tight than that exercised over state departments.

It is generally held that six processes of control over decisions exist in the French administration system:

- The "power of instruction" which consists of giving instruction in advance to subordinates;
- The "power of approval" which exists when a decision can only come into force after approval by the higher authority.
- The "power of suspension" under which a higher authority can defer the entry into force of a decision by the authority beneath it.
- The "power of annulment" under which a decision by the lower authority can be overturned.
- The "power of reformation" under which a decision by the lower authority can be modified.
- The "power of substitution" under which the higher authority can act in the place of the lower one.

Within this general framework control by trusteeship is distinguished from the hierarchic control which exists inside a public service by the following features:

i- Trusteeship may include the last five powers, but never that of instruction.

ii- Trusteeship can never overestimate itself. That is to say, the authority entrusted with the trusteeship (the higher authority) only possesses those among these five powers which the law has expressly conferred on it and only in those matters which the law has expressly laid down. It is a system, therefore, in which the state potentially enjoys more powers than in the system of "local government"; but, in the cases where such a power is not laid down, the state can only annul a decision made by the lower authority by resorting to a judge.

iii- Local authorities can defend themselves against illegal exercise of the power of trusteeship by having the act of illegal control annulled by the administrative judge. (It goes without saying that the same right does not exist for subordinates in the same public service against the control of their hierarchical superior).

3. *Decentralisation and deconcentration*

French local administration is not entirely decentralised. This is indeed far from being the case. Thus, for example, the department is a decentralised group to the extent that it is run by an elected "general council"; but the chief of administration in the department, whose powers are far greater than those of the "general council", is the "Prefect" who is a civil servant and state representative in the department. This administrational process which consists of entrusting far-reaching powers to the local representatives of the central power is known as "deconcentration", which is clearly distinguished from the concept of "decentralisation"; the Prefect is a "deconcentrated" authority, whereas the general council is a "decentralised" one.

One of the basic current problems in French provincial administration is this precise choice between "deconcentration" of the central power and "decentralisation". There are many people who believe that an increase in decentralisation is accompanied by the risk of a dislocation in the unitary state which would be alien to the French tradition. Thus, in financial matters the state remains the main source of public investments; since 1970, it has been possible gradually to confide the choice of investments and determination of priorities to the Prefects. But there has never been any question of entrusting them to the decentralised local authorities. The same is true in the case of planning and the parcelling out of land. Local authorities are at the most consulted so as to provide added information for the choices of the central power.

II   *Some of the current problems in the French system of distribution of administrative jurisdiction:*

1. *Reform of the communes:* The economic, social and political efficiency in the communes in France is becoming lower and lower to the point of reaching an intolerable level for a modern country. Everything results from the fact that there are 37,500 communes in France, 30,000 of which have less than 1,000 inhabitants.

Being a local group with general jurisdiction, the commune provides extremely diversified services (vital statistics, censuses, police, public health, fire prevention, social security, communal roads, provision of water, sanitation, electricity, and public lighting, for example). A decree of 20 May 1955 grants communes the right to intervene in all economic and social domains; but a commune with less than 1,000 inhabitants clearly does not posess sufficient financial means to employ all the powers the law provides it with: the personal resources of the commune are limited to the degree that efficient municipal management is only possible with state subsidies and loans. But in this case local autonomy is only a fiction, since the state naturally maintains tight control over the uses its subsidies are put to.

The force of tradition is such that in spite of significant financial enticements from the state in this direction, and despite the formulation of a sort of national regroupment plan (in application of a law of 16 July 1971), communes will rarely agree to fuse together. On the other hand, several formulas for the association together of communes do currently exist for the purposes of running in common one or several public services. These associations of communes have the legal status of public establishments and can meet the different needs of the urban and rural zones: the "commune syndicates", of limited jurisdiction, have been of real service in urbanised regions, just as they have been in rural ones; the "districts", which have wider jurisdiction, have not had the success hoped of them. Finally, the "urban communities", reserved for multicommunal agglomerations of more than 50,000 inhabitants are stripping the communes which are members of them of almost all their traditional jurisdiction; they could have significant consequences, but are as yet still limited in number.

The foreign observer will perhaps be surprised at this outline (too sketchy) of a system of provincial administration whose archaism is unique in Europe. The reason for this is that no government has envisaged, as in England, a reorganisation imposed by the legislator: by the logic of communal autonomy it has always been considered that the communes themselves should be entrusted with improving provincial structures. This explains why these different types of associations or these fusions cannot be imposed on the communes. One day this voluntary system will probably have to be abandoned.

2. *Regional reform:* A similar problem arises at the level of higher administration: just as the communes are too small, it had long been noticed that the departments created in 1789 had become too restricted an administrational framework for most of the functions assumed by them, but they were particularly too limited to play a useful role in economic development.

The basic feature of the regional institutions created in 1964 and especially by the law of 1972 was their economic vocation: the selection of large public investments in the region and partici-

129

pation in planning and parcelling out of land.

Regional reform has not run into the same difficulties as communal reform. It would have been possible to dissolve the approximately 95 departments and replace them with about 10 or 20 regional entities without encountering local opposition; on the contrary "regionalist" notions would have profited thereby. However, the departments were not dissolved, for at least two reasons:

i) in the first place, the department is a traditional administrative level, which has proved itself on numerous scores; it appeared unnecessary to destroy something which functioned more or less correctly.

ii) Above all, however, too forced a regionalism was resented as creating a threat to national unity, and a risk of dismemberment of the state. The excesses of certain regionalist movements (e.g. in Brittany) accentuated this fear of dislocation of the French nation.

In this general context it was therefore impossible to create new local groups with general jurisdiction at the regional level. This is why, in the system established by the 1972 law the word "region" covers two realities: 1) an administrative district of state economic action (analogous to the English economic planning regions), and 2) a public establishment entrusted with the economic development of the regional district. Thus the French region appears to be a sort of federation, an association of several departments and not a local group superimposed on the department. The status of "public establishment" enjoyed by the 22 French regions leads in particular to the following consequences:

i) the "principle of specialisation" which controls the legal organisation of the public establishments is applied to the region: the region is "specialised" in economic and social development.

ii) the governing bodies are not elected by universal suffrage (which is the case with the "municipal councils" in the communes and the "general councils" in the departments); the "regional council" is composed of the parliamentary members in the region and representatives of the departments and communes; the "Economic and Social Committee", which helps it is composed of representatives of economic, professional, trade union, cultural etc. activities in the region.

iii) the head of the regional public establishment is the

"Regional Prefect" who is quite simply the prefect of the department containing the regional capital; the regional prefect thus simultaneously administers a department, promoted to chief department of the region, and a region. This means that the regional administration is much reduced. Besides, the law goes so far as to prohibit the creation of regional services: the region may not possess any personal resources in the form of goods or personnel; it must use the state services in the main department.

On the other hand, the region has personal financial means at its disposal: a state tax, that on driving licences, has been transformed into a regional tax, and in the future the region will be allowed to supplement its fiscal resources without at the same time exceeding a maximun laid down by the law.

The entirety of the regional taxes is to definitively represent 0.5% of the whole of existing taxes, 10 to 12% of taxation in the communes, and 20 to 24% of departmental taxation. This is to say that financial means in the region are limited: a regional budget can only be a running budget to be concentrated on some investments of local interest. Here we have a useful solution from the economic point of view, but one whose operation presents one serious defect: out of due respect for equality, resources proportional to the population of each region were laid down. This equality threatens to aggravate inequalities between regions: the least populous regions are also the least developed; their resources being limited, they cannot make up their backwardness in comparison with regions which are more populous and therefore richer.

Despite these defects and uncertainties, the reform of 5 July 1972 has the great merit of being supple and forward-looking: the regions can combine and federate to execute an operation of common interest; the state on the one hand, and the departments and communes on the other will in the future have the chance of definitively transferring a part of their jurisdiction (and, naturally, of their resources) to the regions. It is therefore possible that each region will in the future have all its individual personality: region X will have absorbed almost all the jurisdiction of its departments; region Y will have practically no power. This represents a considerable evolution in the French mentality, for it is the first time that the rule of uniformity in provincial administration has been overlooked. Under this rule, for example, a commune of 100 inhabitants could legally have exactly the same sphere of influence as one of 100,000.

3. *Reform of the public establishments*

The final category of corporate body in public law, the public establishments, also raises numerous problems.

The legal form "public establishment" is used nowadays in extremely varied fields. The absence of any coherent administrative doctrines in the creation of public establishments was recently condemned in a report by the Council of State[1]: formerly the creation of a public establishment corresponded solely to the desire to give a legal personality to either a public service (university, hospital), or to a human group (chamber of agriculture). Nowadays very many public establishments are public companies (Electricité de France; Charbonnages de France, French Coal Board) and certain of them even play the role of holding companies (Institute of Oil Research and Activity, mining and chemical company); the formula of public establishment is even used with regard to provincial administration (districts, urban communities, regions) in such a way that pragmatism involves it increasingly with judicial precision which requires a clear distinction to be drawn between public establishment and local group.

This suppleness and pragmatism certainly have numerous advantages: but administrative efficiency and the satisfaction of those administered do not necessarily gain thereby. It can be seen, therefore, that relations between the state and the public establishments are not very clear: "trusteeship tends more towards exhaustive checking of acts of management of the public establishments rather than towards a definition of the objectives of the organisms"[2] In other words, the creation of public establishments does not correspond to a coherent decentralisation policy. Thus, for example, it can be seen that in certain sectors the state provides the quasi-totality of the governing power or police power to a public establishment, but by a sort of counter-balance to this it supervises very closely the daily use this delegation is put to. This is the case with certain professional public establishments. In conditions such as this the question could be mooted as to whether the central power should not rather delegate powers which are more limited, but which the establishment could use more freely; present-day solutions consist too frequently of a par-celling-out of centralisation rather than true decentralisation.

The suggestions for reform from the public establishments generally concur on the following points with the 1971 Council of State report: i) It would be fitting to limit and rationalise the creation of public establishments by investigating in each case whether such a creation in necessary.

ii) The state should define more clearly the role assigned to each public establishment and provide in each case the necessary stimulus for the fulfulment of this role.

iii) The state should allow public establishments a much greater degree of liberty in their everyday running and supervise more rigorously the results of this running.

The problems raised above (administration of communes, regional administration and public establishments) are among the most crucial of those currently facing French administration. The question is not, properly speaking, to improve administrative efficiency: the problem is to reconcile the greatest possible efficiency with the most democracy possible. It is this which is the difficult balance-point to find in each field of administrative action, and the one increasingly necessary to find for the satisfaction of those administered.

Today it appears that the technocratic stumbling block has been clearly recognised: the theme of participation by citizens in administrative action is sufficiently in fashion that it may be hoped this danger is remote. On the other hand, certain examples suggest that an administration which is exaggeratedly "participative" becomes dangerous, first of all because it loses efficiency, and secondly, because this loss of efficiency is acutely resented by its "participants". The problem therefore no longer seems to be the struggle against the excesses of technocracy in the name of democracy, but rather to avoid the excesses of apparent democracy in the name of genuine satisfaction of the democratic spirit, which demands a minimum of efficiency.

NOTES

1. Council of State, "The Reform of Public Establishments", a report submitted to the President of the Republic on 4 March 1971; French Documentation, 1972.
2. Ibid., p.31.

IX DEVOLUTION IN WEST GERMANY

P.D. Dagtoglou *

A. *Some general remarks on different terms and their meaning*

"Devolution" is not a term used in Germany law or politics. But, of course, what is meant by it is known in Germany, too. There are three pairs of terms used in German law and representing three different aspects of devolution.

1. The first one is the antithesis between *federalism and unitarism*. The distinction lies in the degree of political centralism. A federal state is the union of several "member-states" *(Länder* in the traditional German terminology) which cease, as a rule, to be subjects of international law, but keep their character as states, and their political identity within and towards the federal state as such. This means, first, that they have a legislature, executive and judiciary of their own; secondly a civil service and a political leadership of their own; thirdly an autonomous taxing and budgetary power. Finally, a federal court is necessary for the solution of conflicts between the Federation and the *Länder.*

Whether this is fragmentation or integration of government depends on the starting point (but neither fragmentation nor integration are absolute moral values in the sense that they are always good or always bad). A federalisation of Britain would be a fragmentation of government; the federalisation of the independent German states in 1871 was integration. The German Reich remained federal after the First World War and during the Weimar period but it was speedily converted into a unitary state by national-socialism. After the Second World War federalism was re-established in the western part of Germany in a stronger form than in the Weimar Republic.

2. Whereas the decision between federalism and unitarism has

* Professor of Constitutional Law, University of Regensberg

deep constitutional repercussions, the choice between centralisation and decentralisation, or concentration and deconcentration hardly affects the unity of the political power and relates (mainly) to public administration. Both pairs of terms have been taken from French administrative law and do not mean a certain state of administrative structure, but opposite tendencies or principles which are pursued at a given time but can never be thoroughly carried out. On the contrary their advantages and disadvantages should be considered carefully before any major decision on administrative organisation is taken.

The antithesis *centralisation — decentralisation* is more than the complex "central government" and "local government". It also comprises autonomous corporations not on a territorial but a functional basis. One could also use the terms central government and self-government. Centralisation is the tendency to carry out public administration through direct state (central government) authorities. Decentralisation, on the other hand, is the tendency to delegate administrative duties to autonomous bodies controlled by the central goverment. These bodies can be either territorially based (local government) or functionally structured (public corporation). The decision on a territorial basis is also called vertical, the functional decision is also called horizontal. Vertical decentralisation (local government) is guaranteed by Art. 28 of the Federal Constitution. Practical and historical reasons have also led to a considerable horizontal decentralisation and the creation of a large number of autonomous bodies, corporations, foundations etc.

3.   This is true of the terms *concentration and deconcentration,* too. They only concern the structure of central government. Vertical concentration means the tendency to entrust as many administrative duties as possible to the top authority, while vertical deconcentration means their distribution among several lower, particularly local authorities. Horizontal concentration is the concentration of as many administrative duties of the same level as possible on the same authority ("Unity of Administration"); horizontal deconcentration, on the other hand, is their distribution among several special authorities.

B.   *A general description*

West Germany, being a federal state, has one level of power more than a unitary state: the federal and the member-state level.

Within the latter, there is the "deconcentrated" level of regions and the "decentralised" level of municipalities (boroughs and cities). Groups of small municipalities form districts. As each member state *(Land)* determines autonomously its administrative structure there are differences both in structure and terminology due to history and economic conditions. The organisation of the two cities with member state character, i.e. Hamburg and Bremen, as well as West Berlin, has some peculiarities. Of the remaining member states *(Länder)* Saarland has hardly any and Schleswig-Holstein no regions at all. Baden-Württemberg will have no regions as from January 1st 1977.

Devolution in West Germany is thus carried through in three channels: federalism, deconcentration and decentralisation.

1. *Federalism*

As there are practically as many types of federalism as federal states it is probably appropriate to point out the main characteristics of the Federal Republic of Germany: All *Länder* have constitutions, parliaments, executives, civil services, and first instance and appellate law courts of their own. The federal state as such *(Bund)* has a bicameral parliament: the house of directly elected representatives *(Bundestag)* which is the main political and legislative assembly, and a Federal Council *(Bundesrat)* consisting of representatives of the *Land* Governments and having mainly veto powers in the legislative sphere. The *Bundestag* elects the Prime Minister (Federal Chancellor — *Bundeskanzler*) who in turn chooses the ministers and suggests their appointment to the Federal President *(Bundespräsident)*. All, but also only, the last judiciary instance law courts are federal courts. There is a federal administration at the top and, partially, at the mid level but administration at the citizen's level is, as a rule, carried out by the *Länder*. Unlike the United States where federal legislation is implemented by federal agencies in the Federal Republic of Germany federal legislation is, as a rule implemented by *Land* authorities. On the other hand, the Federal Government is by far the most powerful executive and the Federal Parliament passes the largest and most important part of legislation. As the Federal Government disposes of the biggest part of the revenue and assists the *Länder* with their expenditure it is in a position to influence their policies and executives, too. Finally, the hierarchy of the political parties, trade unions, confederations of

137

industry, and other interest organisations ends invariably in the federal capital and strengthens the federal centre of power.

As I describe in my paper on "Federal Conflicts in West Germany" (see *post*, pp. 155-173), the tendency is towards a stronger federal government, not a federal devolution. Whether this trend would be reversed if Art. 29 of the Federal Constitution were implemented and the federal territory were divided in fewer and economically stronger *Länder* is rather doubtful. For federalism is meaningful only if the member states have a historical and political identity of their own. If this is so, a new division of federal territory might make sense economically but it hardly strengthens federalism as a force of devolution.

2. *Deconcentration*

Deconcentration is a form of devolution. This is especially true in regard to the *vertical deconcentration* which relieves the ministries from a great number of small administrative duties and gives them sufficient time to consider broader and long-term problems.

The reforms which have recently been carried out in most of the *Länder* have greatly diminished the number of regions and districts (to less than a half) by creating bigger units. New regions have a population of about 3.5 million and new districts of about 100,000. Boroughs must now have a reasonably high population (e.g. in Bavaria 50,000) in order to be free of district and subject only to regional control.

These territorial reforms had a devolutionary character as they were accompanied by functional reforms, i.e. the delegation of a considerable number of decisions to regional authorities. In Rheinland-Palatinate, for instance, the territorial reform was connected with the devolution of about five hundred different decision-making powers from the ministries to the regions. However, in most of the *Länder* the territorial reform has been carried out but functional reform has not been introduced yet. The reason is that territorial reform does not automatically prepare the ground for functional reform. Problems of personnel and organisation have to be solved first. However, so long as the functional reform fails to come, the territorial reform alone has anti-devolutionary effects.

While vertical deconcentration is generally welcome, *horizontal deconcentration* is met with critical reserve, for it leads to an

138

over-fragmentation of power with repercussions on the simplicity of public administration and perpetual friction and conflicts of jurisdiction. But apart, of course, from the division of government into ministerial departments and the existence of a considerable number of semi-independent federal or *Land* boards and authorities, historical and organisational reasons led to the creation of some federal or *Land* authorities on mid or low level answerable to the different *Land* governments or to the Federal Government. As already pointed out, the Federal Constitution only exceptionally allows the Federal Government to have mid and low level (local) authorities of its own. The Federal Government must normally use the mid and low level authorities of the *Länder*. But it has a full three level administration of its own in some important areas like foreign affairs, post, railways, sea and inland navigation etc.

Most of the mid and low level authorities are, however, *Land* authorities. The most important mid level ones are the general regional authorities with roughly the jurisdiction of the Home Office on regional level. Apart from them there is a number of specialised mid-level authorities responsible for inland revenue, consolidation of farm land, forestry, social security, etc. There is also a considerable number of low level authorities responsible for health, planning permissions, highways, schools, inland revenue, forestry, etc.

3. Decentralisation

Vertical decentralisation, i.e. *local government*, had sunk to insignificance in most parts of Germany by the end of the 18th century. It was reintroduced by the Prussian City Law *(Städteordnung)* of 1808, on the initiative of Baron vom Stein, as a link between citizens and the state. This political aim was frustrated by the Vienna Congress. Another element, the honorary character of all leading work connected with local self-government, was emphasized by another significant reformer, the liberal politician and writer Rudolf von Gneist, who was strongly influenced by English self-government. This element remained characteristic but was never decisive due to the dramatic rise of town population during the 19th century and the enormous increase and specialisation of self-government work. The decisive element lies elsewhere: Self-government means in Germany administration through autonomous corporations.

In a Germany consisting of a great number of principalities and, after 1871, united into a federation, local government developed differently in different areas. But everywhere, local government comprises only the self-government of cities and boroughs, as well as associations of unions and boroughs. Mid level units, i.e. regions, are considered to be local parts of *Land* government, expressing deconcentration but not decentralisation. In other word, mid level units are not autonomous corporations with a legal personality of their own but deconcentrated authorities of central government, not only controlled, but directly led and ordered by the ministries.

The restriction of local government to the self-government of cities and boroughs can be explained if we remember Baron vom Stein's conception of local government as a link between citizens and the state. This idea can only be understood against the background of the antithesis between state (that is the King and his servants) and society (that is mainly the third estate, the burghers) to which absolutism had led. Self-governed boroughs were free boroughs. Stein considered borough administration to be an administration by society as opposed to the administration by the state. This situation changed with the introduction of constitutional monarchy in the middle of the 19th century but the difference between state administration (comprising also the mid level units, i.e. the regions) and communal administration (comprising also districts with several small boroughs) remained a basic one.

It was, and is, counter-balanced by the federal structure of Germany which prevents (since the creation of the Federal Republic) a too powerful centralism. It is also counter-balanced by a strong tradition of borough autonomy, though this is less true in centralised Bavaria. According to art. 28 s.2 of the Federal Constitution, boroughs must be guaranteed the right to regulate on their own responsibility all affairs of the local community within the limits set by the law. Besides local affairs, boroughs are responsible *for all public matters* in their area which law has delegated to them. Central control, however, goes further, when these latter so-called "delegated" matters are concerned; it is not restricted to compliance with law but also affects the way discretion has been discharged.

Boroughs have also the right to issue by-laws, to decide on their personnel, to prepare and carry through town planning, to establish municipal institutions and corporations. Boroughs have also a taxing power of their own guaranteed by the Federal Constitution (Art. 107 s. 6) but restricted to taxes on real property and taxes on consumption and luxury. Besides, they receive a part (1/14) of the income tax revenue (Art. 107 s 5) as well as donations and subsidies from their own *Land*.

As with vertical deconcentration, vertical decentralisation, too, has been reformed. The reform has greatly diminished the number of cities and boroughs by considerably raising the minimum population requirement of local government. In Bavaria there still are self-governed villages with a population of well under 500. These small units of local government have deep historical roots in large parts of Germany. The long tradition of German independent states and autonomous cities, but also the abuse of central power during the Nazi period led to a distrust of concentration and centralisation and the demand that power be divided and distributed and decisions taken on local level. In old Prussia the attitude was the opposite. There, the local proximity of the civil servant to the questions he had to decide was considered to endanger his objectivity. Local, and also social distance were thought to be indispensable as guarantees of independence and integrity. That was the reason for the frequent transfer of Prussian civil servants.

This Prussian attitude had obviously negative sides resulting from the lack of democratic mentality in government and society of Prussia. But, of course, it also had some positive points which are valid in our days, too; corruption in local administration is by no means unknown in Germany. The enlargement of administrative units has however mainly been the result of rationalisation of financial, political and social means, and of the increasingly inter-regional character of many of the modern problems of public administration.

Following the examples of other *Länder*, especially of Baden-Württemberg, the Bavarian territorial reform of 1971 introduced the so-called "administative communities" (*Verwaltungsgemeinschaften*) of adjoining boroughs which, without taking over completely the autonomy of the boroughs, are to be responsible for a number of municipal duties. Small boroughs are encouraged to join such "administrative communities". As from January 1st, 1976, the mid-level authorities entrusted with the control of local self-government will have the power to create *ex officio* such "administrative communities" with a population of about five thousand if through the union the "administrative capacity" of the boroughs is improved. The constituent boroughs should have a population of at least a thousand; smaller boroughs should merge with others. From January 1st, 1976, the merger will be carried out by central government.

The tendency towards bigger units of local government is related in Germany to the same political and economic problems and considerations as in other comparable countries. It is therefore not necessary to go into them. But again, the territorial reform, insofar as it creates viable units whose social costs do not outweigh the additionally gained financial strength, is an important devolutionary factor.

Apart from the vertical there also exists a *horizontal decentralisation* at federal, *Land* and municipal level. Horizontal decentralisation differs from deconcentration insofar as it not only creates specialised authorities but also establishes independent corporations with a legal personality of their own, like the Federal Bank or the corresponding banks of the *Länder*, the Federal Employment Board, the different broadcasting corporations, the (municipal) savings banks etc. Horizontal decentralisation is a form of horizontal devolution.

4. *Private sector*

Apart from the three channels of devolution mentioned above public matters can also be "devolved" to the private sector.

It is not easy to define public matters, and the criteria change from country to country, and from time to time — generally embracing an increasingly wide area. Public matters are basically the domain of government in its widest sense though by no means all public matters are administered by public authorities, boards or corporations. Here again there are considerable differences from time to time, and from country to country. Whereas the medical services are nationalised in Britian, and the area of public ownership is wider than in West Germany (for instance, German steel is private) several other activities of social important character are left in Britain to the private initiative either on a profit or on a charity basis. While most employment agencies are private enterprises in Britain, they are authorities of a federal board in Germany. On the other hand, more than half of the German theatres are national or city theatres. However, wide areas of socially important services are in both countries parts of the public sector: water, electricity, gas, transport etc.

142

If de-nationalisation can be considered as a form of devolution there is very little of it in Germany. The most important case is the Volkswagen works which were transferred in 1961 from the public to the private sector but with decisive government influence on their board. More frequent and practically more important is the supply of certain public services (e.g. postal services) in the form of a public authority or a commercial company, or the supply of these services by the government or local government directly or through a private company employed by the government or local government to this purpose (i.e. building and administration of a harbour or airport, refuse collection and disposal etc.). In Germany this lies in the discretion of the public body responsible for the services affected, and is judged on financial and practical criteria: economic viability and efficiency — hardly devolution. In this way, methods and forms of private business are applied and private companies are widely employed by government. Generally, there has been a tendency to rely on private companies and use them as much as possible. A provision of the Bavarian Local Government Act (Art. 89 s. 1) is characteristic: A borough can only establish or take over an enterprise if, *inter alia*, this is in the public interest *and* the purpose is not, or cannot be, fulfilled just as well and economically by a private enterprise. However, the accepted meaning of "enterprise" in this provision is confined to profit seeking bodies.

C. *Finance*

Finance is the most frequent cause of friction between the Federation, the *Länder*, and the boroughs, as the perpetually expanding welfare state demands increasing expenditure and therefore greater revenue. Federalism or local government would be speedily and effectively undermined if they had not the revenue to meet their needs. The problem is further complicated by the considerable financial inequalities between the different *Länder* and the boroughs. All this is certainly nothing special to Germany but there the federal system complicates the matter even more by providing an additional level and, particularly, by securing a financial and budgetary autonomy for the *Länder* which, on principle, does not allow federal grants to the boroughs, or other public bodies below the *Länder* level.

The Federal Constitution distributes revenue between the Federation, the *Länder* and the boroughs (Art. 104 a *et seq.*). The dis-

143

tribution is a fixed one but there are possibilities of adaptation of the ratio of apportionment, or of equalisation by grant.

Basically, the Federation and the *Länder* each bear the expenditures resulting from the exercise of their respective functions. But whenever a *Land* acts as an agent for the Federation, the Federation bears the expenditure. (Art. 104a ss 1 and 2). In the case of the so-called "common tasks" of the Federation and the *Länder* (building of universities, improvement of regional economic structure, the structure of agriculture, and coastal defence the Federation bears half (or at least half) of the total costs (Art. 91 a). In the field of educational planning and scientific research of national importance the Federation and the *Länder* can again cooperate and agree on the share of the costs (Art. 91b). Finally the Federation can give financial aid to the *Länder* for "particularly important investments" of the *Länder* and the boroughs, necessary for counteracting general economic disturbances, or for equalizing varying economic power in different parts of the country, or for promoting economic growth, e.g. for purposes of national importance, which should not be financed by *Land* or local government alone.

Tax legislation is mostly a federal matter with the main exception of local excise taxes. Revenue from customs duties, taxes and financial monopolies is distributed by the Constitution (Art. 106) between the Federation, the *Länder* and the boroughs in two different ways: either by allocating the revenue of certain taxes to the Federation, the *Länder* or the boroughs, or by apportioning the income from one or more taxes between the Federation, the *Länder* and the boroughs (so-called *Steuerverbund*). Obviously, this latter system applies to taxes rich in yield; Federation and *Länder* share equally the revenue from income tax and corporation tax. The ratio of apportionment of turn-over tax is fixed and, from time to time, modified by federal law, subject to the consent of the Federal Council.

The boroughs' revenue derives from taxes, rates, fees as well as from property income, and grants. The boroughs' tax revenue derives either from certain taxes (especially taxes on real property and local excise taxes) which accrue directly to them, or from their share in certain tax revenues accorded to the *Länder*. In regard to distribution of tax revenue, revenue and expenditure of boroughs are deemed to be *Land* revenue and expenditure. The distribution of tax revenue between the Federation and the *Länder* is called vertical financial equalisation *(verti-*

kaler Finanzausgleich).

As the *Länder* are of different size and financial strength, there also exists an horizontal financial equalisation (*horizontaler Finanzausgleich*). *Land* revenue is thus distributed between the *Länder* according to the population *and* financial capacity of the individual *Länder and* their boroughs. Such revenue equalisation is provided by federal law, subject to the consent of the Federal Council, and may also include federal complemental grants to financially weak *Länder.*

The Constitution not only guarantees revenue but also the fiscal autonomy of the Federation and the *Länder* (Art. 109 s.1); the constitutional guarantee of local government (Art. 28 s.2) also includes the fiscal autonomy of the *Länder.* However, the constitutional amendments of 1967 and 1968 and the statutes which followed (Promotion of Economic Stability and Growth Act, 1967, and Budgetary Principles Act, 1969) introduced ways and means of federal influence on *Land* and borough budgets. Fiscal autonomy is restricted by the requirement of overall economic equilibrium. Federal legislation lays down budgetary principles obligatory for the *Länder* and concerning short term economic policy and a medium-term financial planning. This financial planning, at federal, *Länder* and borough level, restricts the financial autonomy of *Länder* and boroughs. Besides, federal legislation may restrict borrowing by boroughs and impose the obligation on *Länder* and boroughs to maintain interest free deposits in the German Federal Bank as an anti-inflationary measure.

Otherwise, the fiscal autonomy of the *Länder* is far wider than that of the boroughs. For local authorities are restricted in their expenditure by detailed legislation providing for extensive control before and/or after the expenditure takes place. But both *Länder* and boroughs are restricted by the fact that many grants or sharing of cost are for specified purposes (cf. Art. 91a, 91b, 104 a s. 4, Art. 106s. 8 Fed. Const.)

D. *Control by the centre*

The federal structure of West Germany acts as an additional dimension to the control of devolution by the centre.

1. *The control of federal devolution by the federal centre*

According to Art. 28 s. 3 of the Federal Constitution the Federa-

145

tion shall ensure that the constitutional order in the *Länder* shall conform to human rights, the principles of republican, democratic and welfare state and to free local government.

Apart from these general obligations the *Länder* have several other obligations imposed on them either by the federal consitution itself or by federal statutes. The Federation (and that means practically the Federal Government) must make sure that the *Länder* comply with their federal obligations. For this purpose, it disposes of different control mechanisms: a) the federal legislation, b) the so-called federal supervision, c) financial measures, d) legal action, especially action brought before the Federal Constitutional Court, and, e) if everything else fails, the so-called federal enforcement. To explain all these control mechanisms would involve the exposition of a large part of German Constitutional law and cannot be undertaken here — the more so as a federal devolution is, at least *ad nominem*, excluded by the Kilbrandon report.

It should be said, however, that, given the constitutional, political and financial strength of the Federal Government, federal control is most efficient and has never yet had to make use of the radical means of the so-called federal enforcement.

2. *The control of local government by the central Government*

German boroughs administer all local affairs (barring statutory exceptions) as their own affairs. They are also responsible for all other public matters entrusted to them by law. Central control is restricted to the legality of the administration of local affairs, while it extends to a review of discretionary power in regard to the other matters. The way the boroughs spend their revenue and dispose of their assets is also specially and often meticulously controlled either by means of a notification of the intended action, or a permission required *before* the measure is carried out, or by the submission of borough accounts to regional or district audit.

The boroughs have not only the right of complaint but can also bring an action against the supervisory authority before the administrative court. They can also appeal to the Federal Constitutional Court, or the Constitutional Court of their *Land* if they claim that their right of self-government has been violated by a federal or a *Land* law. Central control is least efficient when local bias affects decisions particularly on planning and public works in a way escaping the law. The enlargement of boroughs seeks, *inter alia,* to diminish the danger of local nepotism and corruption.

E. *Difficulties and adequacy*

1. At *federal level,* the difficulties relate to the wish of the people to have and do mutually exclusive things: the demand for a far reaching autonomy but also the demand for equal standards of life throughout the country. The Federal Constitution itself proclaims equal standards of life as a reason for and an aim of, extensive federal legislation (Art. 72 s.2, 75, 105 s.2), or a financial equalisation between the Federation and the *Länder* (Art. 106 s.3 no. 2).

At *local government level* the difficulties relate to another contradiction in the wish of the people: big size and financial viability and strength on the one hand, and proximity and "humanity" of local political power on the other.

2. The question of adequacy cannot be answered with a simple yes or no. It is probably better to ask, *how* to make devolution more adequate. For devolution must be; otherwise, central power will outgrow its usefulness and become an insensitive Leviathan. However, the dimensions of modern administrative problems, and the strength of certain minority groups or multinational companies are too big for small administrative units to cope with; indeed, even national governments find it increasingly difficult to cope with the challlenge. Thus, central government must be too. It is, theoretically, a question of a perpetual balance on a tightrope with much similarity to the desirability and the problems of economic growth. There are however at least the following factors to be taken into account:

a) Financial efficiency cannot be calculated without taking into account the social costs; an unviable unit, though, not only fails to solve, but also creates social problems.

b) Local and national autonomy are limited by national and international interdependence.

c) Federalism does not necessarily guarantee devolution at lower levels. In West Germany, Bavaria is, among all *Länder,* at the same time the most federalist (towards Bonn) and the most centralist (towards its own provinces).

147

X DEVOLUTION IN CULTURAL AFFAIRS IN BELGIUM
K. Rimanque *

A. *Preliminary Observations.*

Till 1970 Belgium was a decentralised unitary state. But its population does not have a common language, nor culture. There
exist two main cultural communities, the Dutch-speaking and
the French-speaking. There is also a German-speaking minority
in the east of the province of Liège, mainly in the districts
annexed after the first world war. These communities live
together in separate parts of the country: Flanders and Wallonia.
In the centre is Brussels, the capital district with about 13% of the
population; the inhabitants of the capital district are in majority
French-speaking (about 75%) and about 25% of its population is
Dutch-speaking.

In the period 1968-1971, the Belgian constitution was
amended, primarily to recognise legally the existence of the cultural and linguistic duality of the Belgian nation. This recognition
has resulted in specific forms of devolution.

The constitution recognises now three *cultural communities:*
the Dutch, the French and the German (section 3 ter). This provision as such is of more political and psychological, than of legal
and institutional value.

The constitution divides the country in *four linguistic regions:*
the Dutch, the French, the German and the bilingual region of
the capital district. The actual boundaries between these regions
are laid down in Acts of 1962 and 1963 as amended by the Act of 23
December 1970. These boundaries can for the future only be
changed by an act of Parliament, adopted with a special majority
of two thirds of the votes, combined with the majority of the votes
of each linguistic group (section 3 bis). As a result no cultural

*Professor of Constitutional Law, University of Antwerp.

community can expand its territory, without the consent of the other; that means in terms of policy that, without mutual concessions, the linguistic boundaries are "frozen".

The cultural duality of the nation is also recognised in Parliament: every elected member of the House of Representatives and of the Senate (every M.P., except Senator Prince Albert) belongs to the Dutch or French-speaking group in Parliament. There is no German linguistic group (section 32 bis). Except for those members elected by bilingual colleges, no member is free to choose a group (act of 3 July 1971, sections 1-3). This division is relevant in the following cases:

a. the constitution of the Cultural Councils;
b. the adoption of acts with a special majority;
c. the admissibility of a motion of one group stating that the draft of a legal provision endangers the good relations between the communities ("alarm"-procedure of section 38 bis of the constitution);
d. the parity between Dutch- and French-speaking Ministers (section 86 bis of the constitution).

The above preliminary observations are necessary for the understanding of the institutional machinery of devolution in cultural affairs. In 1970-71 *cultural autonomy* of the two main cultural communities was introduced in the constitution (art. 59 bis.) and elaborated in the statutes of 3 and 21 July 1971.

B. *The institutions of cultural autonomy: the Cultural Councils*

The constitution has provided two Cultural Councils, one for the Dutch community and one for the French community. The members of the Dutch linguistic group of the House of Representatives and of the Senate form the Dutch Council, and those of the French group of both Houses form the French Council. In fact, the Cultural Councils are parliamentary institutions: there are no separate elections for the Councils; each elected M.P. is *ex officio* member of one of the Councils; they function, some details notwithstanding, as parliamentary institutions.

The Cultural Councils have no executive authority of their own. The central government has not only a right of legislative initiative in cultural affairs; it is also competent to execute the decrees of the Cultural Councils. On the other hand there are in the government two ministers of national education and two ministers of cultural affairs, one for each cultural community. But even these ministers are not responsible to the Cultural Council. The political responsibility of the ministers remains entirely within the discretion of the national Parliament.

The Cultural Councils have no power to levy taxes. The national Parliament decides the global budget of each Cultural Council and gives binding instructions about the portion to spend on the development of each of the cultures in the capital district. Except for these restrictions, the Councils are free to spend their budget on swimming pools, broadcasting, adult-education, theatres, etc. As a result, the Cultural Councils have only normative or legislative competence. On the other hand, the members of the Councils are the M.P.s. It is hard to believe that a minister of cultural affairs could hold office, if he lacked the confidence of a majority in the Cultural Council. Without all its privileges and powers, the Cultural Councils are basically parliamentary institutions.

C. *The powers ratione materiae of the Cultural Councils*

The Cultural Councils have power to legislate in cultural and educational affairs and in the use of languages. The problem is that these subjects are not entirely within their competence and difficult and delicate conflicts may arise with the national Parliament.

The statute of 21 July 1971 contains the list of cultural affairs. These matters are:

a. *The protection and lustre of the language:* e.g. questions of orthography, the promotion of literature at home and abroad, literary prizes and grants, but not the penal code provisions on pornography, the moral protection of children and young persons, economic and tax regulations on the publishing and bookshop business.
b. *The encouragement of the training of scientists:* e.g. scientific grants and scholarships, institutions for the encouragement of scientific research.
c. *Fine arts, music, theatre and movies,* with the exception of all aspects in connection with labour and social security law, penal law and economic regulations.
d. *The cultural patrimony, museums and other scientific and cultural institutions:* e.g. the protection and restoration of historic buildings, important landscapes and reserves, the

establishment and management of museums and other collections.

e. *Public libraries and record libraries.*

f. *Broadcasting, with the exception of the transmission of governmental communications and commercial publicity*: By law broadcasting corporations are not allowed to broadcast commercials. This question remains within the competence of the national Parliament.

g. *Youth-policy*: e.g. subvention of youth-movements, youth-clubs, social promotion, but not instruction nor legislation on the protection of children and young persons.

h. *Adult education and cultural stimulation:* which includes all possible activities in this field, e.g. the question of the foundation of an open university, but not instruction in the traditional sense.

i. *Physical education, sports, camping and caravanning,* with the exception of the regulations on betting, boxing, drugs, and social security.

j. *Recreation and Tourism.*

The Cultural Councils are also competent to regulate *cooperation between the two cultures* (joint committees for cooperation) and for *international cultural cooperation.* But according to the constitution the King has the treaty making power, and for most treaties approval of the national Parliament is necessary (section 68 of the constitution). International treaties, within the sphere of competence of one or both Cultural Councils are approved by the Parliament on a resolution of the Cultural Council or Councils involved.

D. *Power in educational affairs.*

In principle, the Cultural Councils have full competence in educational affairs, with the exception of subjects which the constitution reserves to the national Parliament. In fact most of the important issues of our educational system are kept within the sphere of the national authorities: compulsory education, the structures of instruction, the regulation of certificates (and its consequences on the curricula), financial regulations on school-management, salaries of teachers and professors, and above all, "school-peace", which means every aspect of our school-system, in connection with the delicate political balance between the private or free (mostly catholic) schools and the official schools of the state, provinces or communes. As a result, not much political power is left to the Cultural Councils in this field. The reason for it is that in the national Parliament, there is a balance of influence between catholics and non-catholics but this balance is broken in the Dutch Council in favour of the catholics and in the French Council in favour of the non-catholics.

E. *Competences in linguistic affairs.*

The Cultural Councils also have some competence to regulate the use of languages for some fields of public life: public administration, education in official or state supported schools, labour relations between employers and their personnel, the deeds and documents of enterprises which are prescribed by law. They have no competence to regulate the use of languages in judicial procedures, in the army and for the adoption and publication of acts, decrees and regulations of any authority with normative competence.

F. *The competence ratione loci of the Cultural Councils.*

In this respect, their competence is limited by the constitution. Its extension is not the same for cultural affairs and education on the one hand and for linguistic regulations on the other hand. In general the decrees of each Council have force of law in the Dutch or French linguistic region as the case may be, but not in the capital district, nor in the German linguistic region. But there are many exceptions to this general principle of territorial or institutional origin, e.g. a decree of the Dutch Council about theatres is also binding for the exclusive Dutch-speaking theatres in Brussels, but a decree on the use of languages in the civil services is not applicable to the administration of the national airport at Zaventem (Dutch linguistic region). If neither Council is competent, the national Parliament or the government is. Merely glancing at the competences of the Cultural Councils it is not difficult to see that there is an urgent need for procedures to prevent and to resolve conflicts between the Councils and the national Parliament.

  In this respect, it is most important to note that the decrees of the Cultural Councils have force of law; within their competence *ratione materiae* and *ratione loci* they are equal to an act of Parliament. The decrees can amend or abolish existing laws and regulations. A new act of Parliament cannot be applied within the territory of one of the Cultural Councils when it regulates a subject within the competence of the Councils. But the courts are not authorized to decide these conflicts.

G. Conflicts between acts of Parliament and decrees of the Cultural Councils.

A special procedure is instituted by the law of 3 July 1971 to prevent such conflicts, or, if they should arise nevertheless, to solve them.

Any draft of any law (with the exception of the case of urgent necessity) and any draft of any decree on the initiative of the government has to be submitted for the advice of the legislation section of the Council of State. This body gives advice on the constitutional and legal issues raised by the draft. If the Council of State is of opinion that the draft of a law disregards the competence of the Cultural Councils, there is no sanction; but if it is of the opinion that the draft of a decree exceeds the competence of the Council, this provision cannot be adopted by the Cultural Council unless both Houses of Parliament adopt a resolution stating that the provision concerned does not exceed the competence of the Council. Propositions on the initiative of members of the Cultural Councils may also be subject to the advice of the Council of State. In fact, Parliament is judge in its own cause; the Cultural Councils are in an inferior position.

If a conflict arises in court or before an administrative tribunal as to whether a law or a decree ought to be applied in the case, this prejudicial question is sent to another section of the Council of State, the section of conflicts of competence. However, its decisions are not final. Within a certain time, Parliament can overrule the decision of the Council of State. When such a question arises for the first time before the Supreme Court *(Cour de cassation)*, it is immediately sent to the Parliament for decision. That means that in any case the national Parliament remains the highest and sovereign institution to decide on the constitutional questions of competence of the common legislature and the Cultural Councils. The reason is obvious: traditionally, the Parliament is the highest and only judge of the constitutionality of the law.

XI THE CHANGE IN FEDERAL CONFLICTS

Some remarks on modern West German Federalism

P.D. Dagtoglou *

According to traditional German theory a federal state is marked by a combination of multiplicity and unity; it presupposes a minimum of diversity as well as of homogeneity among its members.[1]

This demonstrates also the traditional theory of conflict: conflict arises from diversity; it is settled on the basis of homogeneity. A basic feature of federal states is that conflicts are not eliminated *a priori;* on the contrary, through the dissimilarity which is inherent in, and cultivated by, the federal state, conflict is both legitimated and accommodated. Indeed, it is an indication that the constitutional structure of the federal state is full of vitality. Yet it is no less essential for a federal state in the interest of promoting the integration of heterogenous elements[2], to create and keep alive the political climate and legal machinery necessary for the solution of conflicts.

I. Uniformity and Federal Conflict

However, in recent years this traditional concept of the German federal state has come under fundamental criticism[3]. The historical and political identity of the German member states *(Länder),* and along with it the objective diversity of the whole nation, have — with few exceptions — vanished irrevocably. These member states and their people had a marked individuality in 1871 when the German *Reich* was founded; they were distinguished from each other by different history, consciousness of their origins, and separate dynasties. Later, though, in two lost wars, and especially in the disaster of 1945, they experienced a common national destiny and a common responsibility. The fall of the old *Länder* (above all the disintegration of Prussia), and the founda-

* Professor of Constitutional Law, University of Regensburg.

tion after the Second World War of new *Länder* by the Allies, flooded moreover with refugees, concealed the differences in origin and mixed them up. Business, pressure groups and political parties alike know no *Länder* boundaries and extend their organisation and activity all over the Federal Republic[67]. The demands of technology, economy, communications and — last but not least — the progressive merger of the economic territories of the European Communities, led to a high mobility of population and at the same time to uniform legal regulations. The welfare state, chiefly the result of war, demands unity and equality[4]. Opinion polls inform us that the demand for stronger powers of the federal agencies are in recent years meeting with considerably more response from the population[5]. The great need experienced in the past, and the present mobility of population has led to a situation where the German citizen is no longer prepared to accept the traditional federal differences between states in taxation, economic growth, education, social services etc.[6]. The Constitution itself provides for "uniformity of living conditions in the federal territory" by expanding federal legislative powers for this purpose[7].

Not that this development is confined to Germany, of course. Very similar trends can be found in American federalism[8]. Sir Kenneth Wheare, whose well-known book on Federal Government[9] deals mainly with the United States, Canada, Australia and Switzerland, identifies four chief forces (war, economic depression, growth of the social services and the mechanical revolution in transport and industry) which have caused central government to increase in strength at the expense of the region (though in my opinion this is not the inevitable result of the growth of social services). He admits, however, that regional governments have also expanded their functions, especially in the sphere of police services, education, health and services for the poor. This is undoubtedly true, though the central government in Germany has to a certain extent expanded in these areas too. However, expansion of the central government is everywhere the chief trend in federal countries. The sense of grievance felt by the regional governments, which according to Professor Wheare leads to a strong increase of self-consciousness and self-assertiveness, does not change the picture; it only demonstrates that in some cases (e.g. Canada) there is hardly an alternative to federalism and that there are some ultimate limits to the expansion of central government. But it does not argue against the expansion as such and what it represents, namely, the progressive deviation from the original concept of federalism in all federal states of our time.

In Germany, these unitary forces are responsible for a massive increase of federal powers and an extensive self-coordination of the *Länder* in the form of recurrent agreements between them (based on mutual compromises) concerning uniform legislative and administrative policy.

The former effect transcends the constitution through the medium of federal grants-in-aid without statutory authorisation (*Fondsverwaltung*) and by cooperation between the Federal Government and the *Länder*[10]. It leads to a transfer of political activity from the *Länder* to the federal level. On the other hand self-coordination of the *Länder* leads to their increasing uniformity[11] Both undermine considerably the individuality and the political substance of the *Länder*. The fact that self-coordination and cooperation are the sole alternatives to a "directive" (i.e. unilateral) coordination through the Federal Government[12] only underlines the inevitability of the unitary process. Even if one were to discount the argument that the diversity of the *Länder* (with the exception perhaps of Bavaria and the Hanseatic townstates of Hamburg and Bremen) was already lost[13], even if one put the accent on "co-operative" federalism as a modern (through formerly not unknown) form of German federal politics[14], one cannot deny two things:

(a) That cooperation as such has unitary effects,[15] and intense cooperation can endanger the autonomy of the member states [16] and considerably supersede *Länder* parliaments,[17] thus resulting in a self-defeat of functional federalism;

(b) Regional individuality and dissimilarity, let alone the consciousness of being a separate people or, even more, a separate state, is vanishing rapidly. Not individuality and diversity, but homogeneity and uniformity dominate increasingly the overall picture of the Federal Republic of Germany.

It is not the purpose of this paper to seek the *raison d'être* of federalism in to-day's Germany[18]. But even if, like the author, one realizes the good, though changed, sense of modern German federalism, one has to reckon with the uniforming realities mentioned above. They indicate that the *main field of conflict between the Federal Government and the member-states does not lie any longer in the variety of its members.* On the contrary, it is the party-political constellations and arguments of expediency

157

which often, if not mostly, decide whether regional differences should be emphasized, put forward or put aside.

Beside the more and more infrequent "genuine" federal conflicts (which are not only formally but also genuinely conflicts about legislative and executive powers [19] , conflicts of a different kind arise increasingly between the Federal Government and the *Länder,* which are not really federal in character. They are *conflicts between different political ideologies* within the whole country or, more correctly, between the political parties in power and those in opposition [20] . We shall return to this development, but must first draw attention to another structural change.

II. Legislative Conflicts

Conflicts between the Federal Government and the *Länder* rarely relate to the exercise of executive or judicial functions. Mostly, they are concerned with the distribution of legislative powers, as when a particular federal or state law is challenged either *per se* or by reference to an administrative or judicial act based upon it. We shall call conflicts of this kind *legislative conflicts.*

The reason for this concentration of federal conflicts into the legislative sphere is first that statutes, as the main instrument of "distributive justice" in a modern welfare-state, tend in political strife to become a kind of apple of the Hesperides. The detailed character of modern welfare laws often transfers the conflict of interests from the sphere of the Executive to that of the Legislature. This transfer has the added effect of tending to make statutes as detailed as possible. Both effects bring about the result that these statutes, which anticipate initiatives and decisions of the administration, provide the explosive material in political controversy, especially in federal conflict.

The second reason for the concentration of federal conflict in the sphere of the Legislature lies in the fact that according to art. 20 section 3 GG the Executive and Judiciary are bound by law. This subordination to the Legislature is, as far as the *Judiciary* is concerned, very extensive — with the important exception that judges are appointed by the Executive. Admittedly the *Executive* does not as a rule need special authority from the Legislature to plan, co-ordinate or provide social services, but even in these fields it is dependent on the often very detailed budgetary decisions of the Legislature.

158

In West Germany the main weight of legislative power does not rest with member states, but quite clearly with the Federal Parliament.

The latter has exclusive legislative power in relation not only to the objects listed in Art. 73 but also to numerous further objects on the strength of various articles of the Constitution. The legislative powers which the Federal Government shares with the *Länder* are defined in Art. 74 and 104 b GG in such a comprehensive way, are extended through Art. 125 GG to such a great part of the law dated before the constitution, and are so generously implemented in practice, that they leave few areas unaffected.

It is true that the Constitution sets limits to the federal legislative power. On the numerous and important matters of so-called "concurrent" legislation the *Länder* can legislate only insofar as the Federal Parliament does not do so; on the other hand the Federal Parliament can legislate according to art. 72 section 2 GG only on matters which cannot be dealt with by one *Land* or without affecting the interests of other *Länder*, or when there is a need for the maintenance of legal or economic unity, especially the uniformity of living conditions.

But the observation of these limits has not been consistently checked by the Federal Constitutional Court, which eventually entrusted it to the basically uncheckable political discretion of the Federal legislator [21].

Likewise the federal power to enact general rules *(Rahmenvorschriften,* literally: "frame-rules") according to Art. 75 of the Federal Constitution is understood and implemented by the Federal Government in an extensive way, as the detailed "general law" on civil servants of July 1st, 1957 proves [22]. Finally the federal legislative field is extended through powers which are assigned to it by the so-called "nature of things" or because they are immediately related to established legislative power. The thirty-one constitutional amendments introduced hitherto also contributed to the key position of the Federal Government in the sphere of the Legislature. Nearly all of them have extended federal powers. This shows the trend which still exists undiminished.

In its answer of March 3, 1969 to a question in the Federal Parliament about the further development of federalism the Federal Government (then a coalition of both big parties) considered the extension of federal powers in further important areas[23] necessary in order to achieve, as far as possible, equal living conditions

159

áll over the Federal Republic. In fact, the constitutional changes of 1969 established substantial new federal powers. The financial reform of the same year, in particular, transferred numerous new powers (not directly related to finance) to the Federal Government. There is even an extension of federal powers in the new so-called "common tasks" (*Gemeinschaftsaufgaben*) of the Federal Government and the *Länder*, i.e. an institutionalised co-operation between the federal and the *Länder* administrations in certain fields[24] .

The Government which followed the elections of 1969 and 1972, a coalition of the Social Democrats with the small Liberal Democratic Party, also intended— at least to the same degree as the previous Great Coalition— to expand federal legislative powers in several fields[25] . The five constitutional amendments enacted since it came to power have pursued that aim. More constitutional amendments of this kind are considered likely, and a more flexible system of distribution of power between the Federal Government and the *Länder* is demanded in order to avoid frequent constitutional amendments[26] .

As federal powers constantly expand and the importance of statutes increases politically in the modern state, the Federal Government exercises its influence on the Executive and the Judiciary of the *Länder,* too. Not only the federal courts but all other courts, which are *Länder* courts, apply mainly federal law and are, of course, guided by the jurisprudence of the federal judiciary, which is the highest judicial instance in the country.

As far as the executive power of the *Länder* is concerned it is, in fact, greatly limited by (a) the increasingly important role of individual rights guaranteed by the Federal Constitution, and (b) the predominant federal legislative power, so that, for this reason too, conflicts between the Federal Government and the *Länder* principally concern the legislature.

(a)   The Federal Constitution guarantees a number of human rights which have been developed by federal jurisprudence into principles considerably limiting administrative discretion[27] . Especially in matters of economic and professional activities, individual property, and equality before the law the *Länder* executives are bound by federal individual rights as interpreted in detail by federal courts.

(b)   As the legislative power of the *Länder* is confined to fewer and fewer areas, the *Länder* mostly implement federal law. This is the starting point of a complicated system of influence exer-

160

cised by the Federal Government on the administration of the *Länder*; it includes among other things (contrary to the American practice) the intensely detailed form of the federal laws, especially laws directly concerning the administration[28] , through which the Federal Government often anticipates the decisions of the administrative authorities of the *Länder*, and, in a way, compensates itself for its deprivation of administrative functions in favour of the *Länder*.[29]

There are many other ways in which the Federal Government exercises influence on the administrations of the *Länder* — ways which are either known to the Constitution (though not necessarily used in its sense); such as the enactment of general regulations or special orders[30] , creation of autonomous federal authorities and public corporations[31] ; or which are *praeter constitutionem* such as direct contact with the organisations of interests which come under the *Länder*'s sphere of administration, circular letters and instructions to secure the uniform exercise of the discretionary power of the *Länder* etc.[32]

In addition to this the Federal Government influences the administration of the *Länder* through numerous "grants-in-aid" schemes *(Förderungsprogramme)* and comparable plans concerning government grants-in-aid for industry, agriculture, universities, scholarships for students etc... They have been called "forms of indirect legislation"[33] because, although they are not issued in the form of a statute but as instructions for the authorities concerned, they affect the citizens in the same way as a law.

The financial reform of 1969 in fact recognised this, and changed the constitution accordingly.[34]

Finally, *medium-term financial planning* should also be mentioned—which was made possible by amending the Constitution[35] . Although each *Land* makes its own financial plan there has to be co-ordination and, therefore, inevitably, some not unimportant concentration of planning and budgeting in the hands of the Federal Government. Given a) this fact (which cannot be explained further here)[36] , b) the extensive influence which the Federal Government exercises on the administration of the *Länder* by means of legislation executed by the *Länder* and checked by the courts, and c) the fact that the courts increasingly review grants-in-aid schemes and examine whether the instructions concerning them are compatible with the constitutional principle of equality before the law[37] the importance of the traditional supervision of the *Länder* administration by the Federal

161

Government decreases a great deal[38] . *It is thus in the Legislature that the most significant potentialities of federal conflict are concentrated*

In the field of the Legislature the dividing line between the Federal Government and the *Länder* seems to be clearer, and the willingness to reach an agreement less frequent. While the agreements between Federal Governments and *Länder* in the field of administration *(Verwaltungsabkommen)* flourish[39] , the so-called "interpretation agreements" *(Interpretations-abkommen)* on legislative jurisdiction are rare, so that the way remains open for conflict.

This rarity is indeed *at first glance* surprising[40] . An explanation can perhaps be found in the consideration that Federal Government and *Länder* see in the present lack of legal clarity a certain freedom of political movement, which to them is more useful than the legal clarity which would be achieved by contractual commitment (without considering the legal doubts as to the limits of such agreements).

III. *Federal Conflicts and the Federal Council*

A twofold development in the structure of federal conflicts has been outlined in the previous pages: on the one hand they tend to concentrate in the field of legislation; on the other hand they are losing to a considerable degree their "genuine" character and are increasingly moving towards the area of party-political confrontation.

Law and political practice provide for certain institutions where federal conflicts are fought out and decided upon. One should mention here first the numerous *committees and boards of federal co-operation and co-ordination,* like the conference of the Federal Chancellor and the Prime Ministers of the *Länder*[41] , or, in practice more important the Legislative Co-ordination Committees on federal and inter-*Länder* level, like the University and School Education Councils[42] , the Economic Development Council[43] , the Financial Planning Council[44] and the (University Expansion) Planning Committee[45] .

Co-operative committees of a different kind, the inter-*Länder*-committees on Prime Minister or Departmental level, are mainly self-co-ordinating instruments of the *Länder*. All these institutions are constituted on the presumption that confrontation or co-operation takes place between federal sub-units as such. It is also true that when, as so often, financial differences arise between the Federal Government and the *Länder,* the solidarity of the latter frequently supersedes the party-political differences of their government though in many other questions which are not of a mainly technical character the political party division tends to prove itself stronger than the division between Federal Government and *Länder.*

The highest instance for deciding conflicts is the *Federal Constitutional Court.* Here too, genuine federal conflicts comparatively seldom reach the Court. More often than not the Court is called on to decide "federal" conflicts which are in reality party-political ones in federal disguise[46] . This was especially clear in the conflict about the concordat of 1933 between the German Reich and the Holy See[47] , the opinion polls on nuclear rearmament[48] , the federal television[49] and also the state subsidies for political parties[50] .

The significance of the co-operative boards and the Federal Constitutional Court for providing an institutionalised arena of federal confrontation can hardly be underestimated. Yet both belong to a pattern of settling federal conflicts which is, despite differences, not unfamiliar to other federal countries. What one could, however, call a West German peculiarity is the so-called Federal Council *(Bundesrat)* whose consent is necessary for the majority of federal laws. This federal assembly of representatives of *Länder* Governments is the institution in which both already stated phenomena — the structural development of federal conflicts towards a party-political confrontation, and their increasing concentration in the legislative field — can be clearly observed.

The Federal Council is the federal organ through which the *Länder* participate in the federal Legislature and Executive (Art. 50, 51 Fed. Const.). Legally, the Federal Council is a federal assembly based not on party-political constellations (as is the Federal Parliament) but on the division of the Federal Republic in *Länder.* Politically, however, the Federal Council is much more a *representation of the Länder against the Federal Government* than a federal organ expected to pay special consideration to the interests of the *Länder.* The present emphasis differs from the function intended by the fathers of the Federal Constitution.

At the same time the political reality of the Federal Council seems to deviate from its original constitutional conception in a reverse way: by becoming an arena of party-political confrontations regardless of *Länder* boundaries[51] . This antithesis is resolved through a partial development of the Federal Council towards a "Third Level", somewhere between Federal Government and *Länder*[52] . This development is related to the structural changes in federal conflicts.

As it was pointed out earlier, the Federal Government is the centre of legislative power. The tendency is to make this centre even stronger than it already is. It is true that in practically all cases of transfer of *Länder* legislative power to the Federal Parliament the Federal Council is given the right of consent. In the same degree in which the *Länder*, as autonomous member-states, had to give way to the growing importance and the increasing amount of federal legislation, they seek through the channel of the Federal Council to secure influence on the making of federal laws which are of importance to them. In so far as the Federal Council has the right of consent (and, therefore, the right of veto) no federal law can pass against its will. As the Federal Council consists of members of all *Länder* Governments this solution seems to represent a fair compensation, leaving the confrontation between the Federal Government and the *Länder* virtually unaffected and only shifting it from one arena to another. Closer observation reveals, however, a considerable change in the structure of the federal conflicts and federalism in general.

Contrary to drafts suggesting a departure from the rules of the Weimar Constitution of 1919 and the entrusting to the Federal Council of an extensive right of consent[53] the Federal Constitution confines this right to certain cases specifically mentioned in its provisions. As a rule, it only provides for a right to "object" to the new law, with a merely suspensive effect[54] . In reality, however, this rule-exception-relation is reversed. The Federal Council's consenting power has been expanded both through constitutional amendments and, in particular, through a remarkably extensive interpretation of Art.84 section 1 of the Federal Constitution[55] . Today more than sixty per cent of the laws, and an even higher percentage of the important ones, are dependent on the consent of the Federal Council.

This development is significant in many ways. Firstly, the *Länder* parliaments lose power both to the Federal Parliament and the *Länder* Governments[56] . The Federal Parliament increases its legislative power at the expense of the *Länder* Parliaments. On the other hand, the Federal Council, whose right of consent increases simultaneously with the increase of federal legislative

164

power, consists only of *Länder* Government (not Parliament) representatives.

This is not the only case in which the shifting of power from the *Länder* to Bonn results in weakening the Parliaments and strengthening the Governments of the *Länder*: the new Art. 91 a s.4 subs. 1 Federal Constitution and the acts of parliament implementing it, provide for a federal share in financing the performance of the so-called "common tasks" (i.e. activities entrusted by the Constitution jointly to the Federal Government and the *Länder*):

This partially federal financing (at least fifty per cent of the total costs) presupposes that the scheme has been included in an outline plan which is approved by a Planning Council consisting of members of the federal and the *Länder* governments. Parliaments do not participate. Federal law provides that all participating governments will take account of the scheme in their budget. Parliaments have formally the right to refuse approval of the necessary expenditure (Art. 91 a s.4 subs. 4 Federal Constitution) but if they do so the federal contribution would be lost. Parliaments are, to all intents and purposes, presented with a *fait accompli* and have no practical alternative but to give their consent. It must be noted though that there are already agreements in some *Länder* on participation of the parliaments.

However, strengthening the position of the *Länder* Governments does not necessarily mean strengthening the position of *Länder* as such. In fact, (and this is the second point) if *Länder* legislative power is increasingly shifted to Bonn and virtually shared by the Federal Parliament on the one hand and the *Länder* Governments collectively (in the form of the Federal Council) on the other it is clear that the *Länder* as such are the losers. For they only share now what they completely (at least legally) possessed before. Even less than that; because the Federal Council decides through the majority of its votes, the minority — let alone the individual *Land* — can be outvoted. The fact that in reality individual, especially the small *Länder* do not completely lose influence is due, apart from the obvious and permanent political bargain, mainly to the Republic-wide party-political allegiance and solidarity — much less to guarantees of the federal system.

The third point refers to the position of the Federal Council. It has become a kind of a federal clearing bank; the federal conflicts are settled within it. The confrontation is not between *Land* and Federal Government but now mostly between the latter and a

165

body which, in political reality, is less federal than was intended and less *Länder*-minded than its composition would suggest. For it represents in a recently increasingly striking way a particular combination of federal traditionalism and party-political unitarism with the latter element apparently gaining ground over the former. At the same time the celebrated "objectivity" and "expertise" of the Federal Council[57] seems to give way to a primarily party-political confrontation. The fact that federalists in politics and theory[58] have been opposed to this development has not stopped it.

This development, it is true, cannot be clearly seen in the statistics. In the first five legislative periods (1949 - 1969) the Federal Council rarely refused its consent[59] ; it even more seldom made use of its right to "object" to federal bills[60] . But also, after the change of Government following the elections of 1969, the overall statistical picture hardly altered[61] . The reason for this seemingly docile behaviour of the Federal Council is certainly not the weakness of its position[62] but, on the contrary, the fact that it can mostly carry its point either directly, or through the so-called Mediation Committee *(Vermittlungsausschuss)*[63]. This is mainly due to three reasons. First, of course, to the power which goes hand in hand with the right of consent, and which forces the Federal Parliament and Government to pay due consideration to the wishes of the Federal Council even during their deliberations; secondly, to the superior administrative experience of the *Länder* bureaucracies which back the Federal Council; thirdly (and perhaps mainly) to the use of its power in a way influencing but not (at least openly) obstructing the Federal Government.

It has always been argued that this delicate structure of legislative co-operation between the Federal Council and the Federal Parliament would very probably soon collapse if an opposition which has the majority of votes in the Federal Council should seek to overthrow the Federal Government by systematic obstruction of its legislative work. The time of trial came after the change of Government which followed the elections of October 1969. The differences between Government and Opposition parties became increasingly overt and sometimes intransigent. They were fought not only in the Federal Parliament but also in the Federal Council, where the opposition secured the majority of votes. The considerable increase in the bills which the Federal Council declared as needing its consent[64] , and especially the sharp rise of the number of cases in which the so-called Mediation Committee was called upon,[65] are probably not without significance in this context. Federal conflicts retreated, by comparison, into the background.

Whether the Federal Council should consider only "federal" or also party-political arguments in its decisions is hardly a question of constitutional law. Forbidding party-political considerations would certainly not make very much sense in the framework of a constitutional law based on the party system[66].

And yet, this development signifies, and of course results from, the gradual transformation of the federal (especially legislative) conflict to a (unitary) party-political one.

This can only mean another important step towards a further weakening of West German Federalism.

NOTES

The following abbreviations are used in the text and notes: AöR:Archiv des öffentlichen Rechts (legal periodical); BGBl I:Bundesgesetzblatt, Erster Teil (Federal Statutes, Part I); BVerfGE: Entscheidungen des Bundesverfassungsgerichts (Decisions of the Federal Constitutional Court); BVerwGE: Entscheidungen des Bundesverwaltungsgerichts (Decisions of the Federal administration Court): DÖV: Die öffentliche Verwaltung (legal periodical; DVBl: Deutsches Verwaltungsblatt (legal periodical); GG: Grundgesetz (Constitution of West Germany; literally: Basic Law); GMBl: Gemeinsames Ministerialblatt (Ministerial Decisions).

1. Carl Schmitt, Verfassungslehre, 3rd ed. 1928, reprinted 1966 p. 375; Peter Werner, Wesensmerkmale des Homogenitätsprinzips und ihre Ausgestaltung im Bonner Grundgesetz 1968.
2. Rudolf Smend, Verfassung und Verfassungsrecht, 1928, now included in: Staatsrechtliche Abhandlungen, 2nd ed. 1968, pp. 119 et seq. (225, 270).
3. See mainly K. Hesse, Der unitarische Bundesstaat, 1962, especially pp. 12 et seq.; also in: Grundzüge des Verfassungsrechts der Bundesrepublik Deutchland, 5th ed. 1972, pp. 88 et seq. (90 et seq);
4. On this question see also W. Grewe, Antinomien des Föderalismus, 1948, pp. 21 et seq.;A. Köttgen, Der soziale Rechtsstaat, in: Festgabe für H. Muthesius, 1960, p. 23; U. Scheuner, Struktur und Aufgabe des Bundesstaates in der Gegenwart-Zur Lehre vom Bundesstaat, DÖV 1962, pp. 641 et seq. (645); Kl. Obermayer, Krise und Bewährung des Föderalismus, in: Neue Ordnung, 1965, pp. 20 et seq., (24 et seq).
5. See the answer of the Federal Government of March 20, 1969 to the question put in the Federal Parliament on June 27, 1968 by forty one MPs on the further development of the federal system. Question and answer are printed

in the Parliamentary Papers (Bundestags-Drucksache) V/3099 and V/4002 pp. 3 et seq correspondingly. The answer is also printed in the publication "Schwarz auf Weiss" of the Minister of the Interior No. 2'68. For a critical commentary on the answer of the Federal Government see P. Lerche Aktuelle föderalistische Verfassungsfragen, 1968.

6. U. Scheuner, Wandlungen im Föderalismus der Bundesrepublik DÖV 1966, pp, 513 et seq. (517); id., Das Bakenntnis des Grundgesetzes zum repräsentativen Prinzip und zum Föderalismus als verfassungsrechtliches Problem, in: A Hollerbach/U. Scheuner/W. Strauss, Totalrevision des Grundgesetzes? 1971, pp. 25 et seq (37/8).

7. See Art 106 section 3 no. 2 GG as it has been amended in the course of the Financial Reform of 1969. See also Art. 72 section 2 no. 3 GG.

8. See for instance W.H. Bennett, American Theories of Federalism, 1964, pp. 197 et seq.

9. K. C. Wheare, Federal Government, 4th ed. 1963 (reprinted 1967).

10. Cf. recently W. Hempel, Der demokratische Bundesstaat, 1969 pp. 21 et seq. with detailed references to further literature. On the subject of the federal grants-in-aid in Germany A. Köttgen's study on "Fondsverwaltung in der Bundersrepublik" 1965, is the standard book (cf. especially pp. 38 et seq. on the aspects related to the separation of powers through federalism). On co-operation between Federal Government and Länder, self co-ordination of the Länder and the grants-in-aid of the Federal Government s. Kommission für die Finanzreform, Gutachten über die Finanzreform in der Bundesrepublik Deutschland (so-called Troeger-Report) 1966, nos. 28-51.

11. Cf. Hesse, Der unitarische Bundesstaat, pp. 20/1

12. Cf. G. Kisker, Kooperation im Bundesstaat -Eine Untersuchung zum kooperativen Föderalismus in der Bundesrepublik Deutschland, 1971, pp. 3. 148, 166.

13. W. Weber, Spannunger und Kräfte im westdeutschen Verfassungssystem, 3d ed. 1970, pp. 228 ff (292 et seq) K. Hesse, Der unitarische Bundesstaat, p. 12.

14. Cf. e.g. Th. Maunz, Deutsches Staatsrecht, 18th ed. 1971 p. 218/9; cf. also the Troeger-Report Nos. 76, 77; G. Kisker op. cit. Kooperation im Bundesstaat - Eine Untersuchung zum kooperativen Födenlismus in der Bundesrepublik Deutschland 1971, with reference to further literature.

15. Cf. K. Hesse, Aspikte des kooperativen Föderalismus in der Bundesrepublik, in: Festschrift für Gebhard Müller, 1970, pp. 141 et seq (145 et seq.)

16. Cf. G. Kisker, op.cit. pp. 135 et seq.

17. Cf. id. pp. 120 et seq; the loss of power of Länder parliaments as a side-effect of modern development of federal co-operation and confrontation will be analysed under III.

18. For a summary on the raisons d'être of the federal state in present day Germany see- P. Lerche, Aktuelle föderalistische Verfassungsfragen, 1968, pp. 9 et seq. with reference to further literature; see also H. Liebrecht, Zur Rechtfertigung des Föderalismus heute und den zu Grenzen zulassiger Kooperation, DVBl, 1969, pp. 47 et seq.; W. Thieme Föderalismus im Wandel, 1969, pp. 148 et. seq.

19. E.g. the conflicts about legislative power in town planning (BVerfGE vol. 3 pp. 407 et seq.) or in water conservation and water roads (BVerfGE vol.

15, pp. 1 et seq) etc.

20. Cf. K. Hesse, Der unitarische Bundesstaat, p. 9, and in: Verfassungs-recht, p. 108 et seq.

21. The judgement of the Court of July 15, 1969 (BVerfGE vol. 26 pp. 338 et seq., especially pp. 382/3) speaks of "political pre-decision" of the Legislature, which in principle has to be respected by the Federal Constitutional Court. In the judgements of April 22, 1953 (BVerfGE vol 2 pp. 213 et seq. esp.224/5) and December 1, 1954 (vol. 4 pp. 115 et seq. esp. pp. 127/8) the Court speaks of discretionary decisions which in principle cannot be reviewed by the courts; in the judgement of November 29, 1961 (BVerfGE vol. 13 pp. 230 et seq. esp. pp. 233 et seq.) the court even refers to the so-called "uncertain concepts" to be found very often in the text of statutes (e.g. "public interest", "necessary measures" etc.) and needing "concretisation", subject in principle to judicial review. This latter opinion is shared by P. Lerche, Aktuelle föderalistische Verfassungsfragen, 1968, p. 23 footnote 48, and N. Achterberg, Die Entscheidung über das Bedürfnis für die Bundesge-setzebung (Art. 72 section 2 GG), in: DVBl. 1967, pp. 213 et seq, who sug-gests that the Federal Constitutional Court ought to exercise its checking powers. But the Court does not show any signs of moving in this direction; in its mentioned judgement of November 29, 1961 (BVerfGE vol. 13 pp. 230 et seq., esp. p. 234) it speaks eventually of a "discretionary field," of the fed-eral Legislator.

22. See the judgement of the Federal Constitutional Court of December 1, 1954, BVerfGE vol. 4 pp. 115 et seq. (128).

23. Education, public health, water conservation, measures against air pol-lution, noise abatement, supervised industries, social legislation, unifica-tion of administrative procedure, organisation of public administration, data processing, salaries of civil servants, and police powers.

24. Art. 91 a, 91 b GG.

25. See the speech of the Federal Minister of Interior, in: Bulletin edited by the Presse- und Informationsamt der Bundesregierung, 1971, No. 3, p. 17, see also: Arbeitsprogramm der Bundesregierung zum innenpolitischen Vor-haben, in: Bulletin, 1971, No. 38 pp. 381 et seq. (400/401).

26. Cf. U. Scheuner, Das Bekenntnis des Grundgesetzes, loc. cit., p. 40.

27. Ibid., p. 38.

28. Cf. Fr. Scharpf, Die Politischen Kosten des Rechtsstaates 1970 p. 53, points out the difference which exists here between Germany and USA.

29. W. Weber, op. cit. p.302; P. Lerche, Aktuelle föderalistische Verfassungs-fragen, p. 17.

30. Art. 84 sections 2 and 5 Federal Constitution.

31. Art. 87 section 3 Federal Constitution.

32. A. Köttgen, Der Einfluss des Bundes auf die deutsche Verwaltung, in: Jahrbuch des öffentlichen Rechts, 1954, pp. 67 et seq. (89/90, 142/3) and: Fondsverwaltung in der Bundesrepublik 1965, pp. 38 et seq.; K. Hesse, Der

unitarische Bundesstaat, pp.17 et seq.; W. Weber, op. cit. pp. 307 et seq.; R. Herzog, Zwischenbilanz um die bundesstaatliche Ordnung, in: Juristische Schulung, 1967, pp. 193 et seq. (107) — However, the checking influence of the Federal Council should not be underestimated; cf. the complaints of the Federal Government in its answer of May 20, 1969, nos. II 4, 3, 4 and 7.

33.   M. Bullinger, Die Zustandigkeit der Länder zur Gesetzgebung, DÖV 1970 pp. 761 et seq., 797 et seq. (pp. 769 et seq.) The problem exists, of course, in the USA too; cf. W. Kewenig Kooperativer Föderalismus und bundesstaatliche Ordnung — Bemerkungen zur Theorie und Praxis des kooperativen Föderalismus in den USA unter besonderer Bërucksichtigung der grants-in-aid in der Bundeshilfeprogramme, AöR 1968, pp. 433 et seq., with reference to American literature.

34.   In the new Art. 104 a section 4 subsection 2 GG. On the whole subject in detail: M. Bullinger, p. cit 770.

35.   Fifteenth Amendment of June 8, 1967 (BGBl, p. 1477), Twentieth Amendment of May 15, 1969 (BGBl I, p. 357); see also the law on Promotion of Stability and Growth of the Economy (so-called Stability Law) of June 8, 1967 (BGBl I, p. 582).

36.   See K. M. Hettlage, The problem of Medium-term Financial Planning, in: Public Administration, 1970, pp. 263 et seq., P. Dagtoglou, Fiscal Policy and Regional Autonomy: Some Constitutional Aspects in Economics, Tokyo, (in press) with further references.

37.   Cf. the judgement of the Federal Administrative Court of April 16, 1969 in BVerwGE vo. 32 pp. 16 et seq (Instructions on granting of scholarships to university students). More details: M. Bullinger, op. cit. pp. 770, with reference to literature and jurisprudence.

38.   In R. Herzog's opinion (op. cit. p. 197) it has even become practically almost superfluous. However, here too one should not underestimate the checking influence of the Federal Council; cf. W. Geiger, Missverstandisse um den Föderalismus, 1962 p. 20.

39.   R. Grawert, Verwaltungsabkommen zwischen Bund und Landern in der Bundesrepublik Deutschland, 1967, pp. 299 et seq. lists 216 agreements; this number should have been considerably increased since then.

40.   W. Rudolf, Bund und Länder im aktuellen deutschen Verfassungsrecht, 1968, p. 34.

41.   Cf. s 31 of the Standing Orders of the Federal Government of May 11, 1951 (GMBl 1951 pp. 137 et seq.)

42.   Wissenschaftsrat (Agreement of September 9, 1957, GMBl 1957, pp. 553 et seq.)- Deutscher Bildungsrat (Agreement of July 17, 1965, Annex A 11 of the Parliamentary Paper — Bundestagsdrucksache — V/2166).

43.   Konjunkturrat (s 18 of the Law on Promotion of Stability and Growth of the Economy of June 8, 1967, BGBl. I 1967 pp. 582 et seq.)

44.   Finanzplanungsrat (s 51 of the Law on Budgetary Principles of August 19, 1969, BGBl I 1969 pp. 1273 et seq.)

45.   Planungsausschuss (s 7 of the Law on New University Building of September 1, 1969, Bgbl I, 1969, pp. 1556 et seq.).

46.   Cf. K. Hesse, Der unitarische Bundesstaat, p. 9, and in: Grundzüge des Verfassungsrechts, p. 108 et seq.

47.   Judgement of March 26, 1957, (BVerfGE vol. 6, pp. 309 et seq.) In this case the (Christian Democrat) Federal Government sued the (Social Democrat) Government of the Land Lower Saxony for violating (through passing a School Law) the Concordat between the Holy See and the German Reich of July 20, 1933, and thereby infringing the right of the Federal Government that international treaties concluded by, and binding it are respected by the Länder The Federal Constitutional Court dismissed the case. Cf. E. McWhinny,, Federal Constitutional law and the treaty-making power. Conflict between legislation passed by member state of federation and treaty obligations of federal government. German-Vatican-Concordat 1933. Decision of West German Federal Constitutional Court, In: Canadian Bar Review, 1957, pp. 842-848.

48.   Judgement of July 30, 1958 (BVerfGE vol. 8 pp. 122 et seq.): The (Christian Democrat) Federal Government sued the (Social Democrat) Government of the Land Hesse for violating its duties towards the Federation by not intervening against decisions of Hessian municipalities to organise official opinion polls on nuclear weapons in the Federal Republic of Germany. The Federal Constitutional Court granted the action.

49.   Judgement of February 28, 1961 (BVerfGE vol. 12 pp. 205 et seq.): The (Social Democrat Government ("senate") of the Land Hamburg sued the (Christian Democrat) Federal Government for creating a Federal Television Company and acting thereby contrary to the Federal Constitution. The Federal Constitutional Court granted the action. Cf. G. Doeker, West German Federal Republic: Television competence, in: AJCL vol. 10, 1961, pp. 277-281.

50.   Judgement of July 19, 1966 (BVerfGE vol. 20 pp. 56 et seq.): The Social Democrat(Government of Hesse requested the Examination of the constitutionality of the Federal Budget Law of 1965 (passed by a Federal Parliament with Christian Democrat majority) as far as it granted state subsidies to political parties. The Federal Constitutional Court declared financing of political parties as being against the constitution — with the important exception of grants-in-aid covering the costs of electoral campaigns. Cf. G. Casper, Williams v. Rhodes and public financing of political parties under the American and German Constitution, in: The Supreme Court Review, 1969, pp. 271-302.

51.   See infra.

52.   Whether this "Third Level" is the same as the so-called "dritte Ebene" of federal agreements cannot be discussed here; on the question of the "dritte Ebene" generally see G. Kisker, Kooperation im Bundesstaat, 1971, pp. 236 et seq., with reference to further literature.

53.   B. v. Doemming/R.W. Fusslein/W. Matz, Entstehungsgeschichte der Artikel des Grundgesetzes, in: Jahrbuch des öffentlichen Rechts,1951, pp. 1 et seq. (615 et seq.).

54. Art 77 Section 3 and 4 Federal Constitution; s 30 section 1 of the Standing Orders of the Federal Council of July 1, 1966, BGBl I, 1966 pp. 437 et seq.

55 BVerfGE vol. 8 pp. 274 et seq. (294); P. Lerche, Aktuelle föderalistische Verfassungsfragen pp. 39 et seq., speaks of a constitutional change through extensive interpretation of the constitution.

56. See W. Leisner, Schwächung der Landesparlamente durch grundgesetzlichen Föderalismus, DÖV 1968, pp. 389 et seq. (especially p. 390); cf. also P. Lerche, Aktuelle föderalistische Verfassungsfragen, 1968, p. 49; K. Hesse, Aspekte des kooperativen Föderalismus in der Bundesrepublik Deutschland, in: Festschrift für Gebhard Müller, 1970, pp. 141 et seq.; A. Böhringer, Zur Mitwirkung der Landesparlamente im Bereich der Gemeinschaftsaufgaben, in Zeitschrift für Parlamentsfragen, 1970, pp. 173 et seq.; H. C. F. Liesegang/R. Plöger, Schwächung der Parlamente durch den kooperativen Föderalismus, DÖV 1971, pp. 228 et seq.

57. Cf. the former President of the Federal Council and later Federal Chancellor K. G. Kiesinger, Gedanken zur Arbeit des Bundesrates, in: Gedächtnisschrift Hans Peters, 1967, pp. 547 et seq.

58. Cf. H. Ehard, Aufgabe und Bewährung des Bundesrates, in: Föderalistische Ordnung, ed. by A. Süsterhenn, 1961 p. 95 (107), 111 et seq.; Th. Maunz, in: Th. Maunz/G. Dürig/R. Herzog, Das Grundgesetz, Kommentar, Art. 50 No. 25, 26.

59. Of 2395 bills passed by the Federal Parliament during its first five parliamentary periods (1949-1969) 1488 (i.e. 62.1 per cent) needed, in the opinion of the Federal Council, its consent, but only nineteen were refused it; cf. G. Ziller, Zwanzig Jahre Bundesgesetzgebung — Die Tätigkeit von Bundestag und Bundesrat im Spiegel der Zahlen — Eine statistische Dokumentation zur Arbeit der gesetzgebenden Körperschaften, in: Bulletin des Presse-und Informationsamtes der Bundesregierung, 1969, No. 113, pp. 963 et seq. (965).

60. In the period between 1949 and 1969 the Federal Council "objected" to federal bills only five times (in the two last legislative periods not at all). On three of these five occasions Federal Parliament modified the bills according to the wishes of the Federal Council; see Ziller, op. cit., pp. 965 et seq., table 6.

61. Of 232 bills passed by the Federal Parliament during 1970 and 1971 161 (i.e. 69.3 per cent) needed, in the opinion of the Federal Council, its consent, but only two were originally refused. In the same period the Federal Council "objected" only to one bill which, nevertheless, became law after a new majority vote in the Federal Parliament. (Information given to the author by the Press Office of the Federal Council on June 28, 1972).

62. Cf. A. J. Heidenheimer, Federalism and Party System — The Case of Western Germany, in: The American Political Science Review, Vol LII (1958) pp. 809 et seq.

63. Art. 77 Federal Constitution; this committee consists of members of the Federal Parliament and the Federal Council and is convened in case of disagreement between these two assemblies. Its propositions can be overruled

by Federal Parliament under more difficult conditions but are usually accepted.

64. During the first twenty years of the Federal Republic (1949-1969) the average percentage of bills dependent on the consent of the Federal Council was 62.1 after the elections of 1969 it rose to 69.3 (see notes 59 and 66).

65. The Mediation Committee was convened in 1970 five, in 1971 eighteen times. (Information given to the author by the Press Office of the Federal Council on June 28, 1972).

66. Cf. H. H. Klein, Parteipolitik im Bundestat? DÖV 1971, pp. 325 et seq.

67. The Bavarian Christliche Soziale Union (C.S.U.) is a notable and peculiar exception.

XII DEVOLUTION OF GOVERNMENT IN SOCIAL SECURITY — SOME EUROPEAN EXPERIENCE.

J. Van Langendonck *

Introduction

It may come as a surprise for the specialists in public law to find "social security" among the subjects for discussion at a symposium on the devolution of government. It probably has never been done before. Very few people will have thought of social security as part of the structure of government.

In fact it is not until recently that social security was looked upon as a direct responsibility of the state. In the 19th century the public authorities only had to organize a system of public assistance to the indigent, and even that obligation was widely questioned as to its extent, its motives and it ways of application[1]. In the first half of the 20th century there has been a great political debate in all countries on the point whether the state had the obligation to solve the "social problems". Henri Hatzfeld has described in an admirable way the French debates on this issue[2], and similar discussions are found in the other continental countries as well, including Germany, where Bismarck had already founded a state social insurance system as early as 1884[3].

The recognition of social security as a state responsibility has come to us with the second world war. The Germans having claimed the superiority of their social insurance, the plans for comprehensive social security systems became part of the psychological warfare. The allied nations, wanting to give the people something to fight for, included social security with the primary objectives to be realized post-war[4].

And so it was. Immediately after the war nearly all countries reorganised their social insurance programmes into a more or less general and more or less comprehensive social security sys-

* Professor of Social Security Law, Universities of Leuven and Antwerp.

tem, which was considered as the realization of the nations' obligation to take care of the social risks for all their inhabitants, freeing them from want and fear[5].

Consequently one sees the post-war constitutions of states declaring, more or less explicitly, the right of all citizens to social security. The preamble to the French constitution of 1946 states that "each human being who is unable to work for reasons of age, physical or psychic condition or economic circumstances has the right to receive from the community a decent living". The Italian constitution of 1947 says, among other things: "the workers are rightfully to expect that measures will be taken to provide them a living in the case of accident, illness, disability, old age or unemployment" and "each citizen who is unable to work and deprived of means of existence has a right to maintenance and assistance" (art. 38). The Luxemburg constitution completed in 1948 contains the phrase: "the system of social security is organized by the law". And the German constitution of 1949 declares the federal republic a *sozialer Rechtsstaat* and attributes the power to organize social security, including unemployment insurance, to the federal government (art. 28 and 74)[6]. Moreover the right to social security was included in the Universal Declaration of Human Rights by the United Nations, of 10 December 1948 (art. 22 and 25)[7].

Once social security was admitted to the rank of government duty, it became a preferential field for devolution of power. No government seemed anxious to deal directly with the collecting of the money or with the distributing of the benefits. This would always be entrusted to specialized institutions, more or less directly derived from the old private funds that had been active in this field. The governments wanted to profit from the experience of these funds in the administrative problems of social security, generally considered as very complicated[8]. They also wanted to leave the social security funds in the hands of the interested groups (mainly employers and workers' unions), because the funds held considerable vested interests[9]. Another reason may have been that they were afraid of a too high expansion of the state budget if social security funds were included; they represent between 10 and 20% of the national income in these countries[10].

The Comparisons

Nothing could be more tedious than an enumeration of the var-

176

ious institutions that are charged with the administration of social security in various countries. They are numerous and diverse beyond imagination. It would be like reading a telephone directory. Yet, something should be said about the actual organisation of social security in a number of countries before this subject can be discussed any further. I propose to concentrate on a few general outlines of the systems in Belgium, the Netherlands, Germany, France and Italy and to deal especially with three topics — (a) division of the institutions by personal and material criteria, (b) role of the institutions and (c) their legal position.

A. Belgium

In Belgium there are two main systems of social security: one for the employed workers, originating in 1944, the other for self-employed, of more recent date — 1967. In the workers' insurance, coal-miners and seamen as well as railway personnel have conserved their own regulations and their own institutions, but for the remainder one can say that there is a large and comprehensive system for all wage-earners.

These institutions are divided by branch of insurance, according to a principle of specialisation[11]. The collecting of the contributions is considered as a specific function and administrated by one central institution. There are separate institutions for the delivery of benefits in the case of industrial accident, of occupational disease, of sickness or disability, of unemployment, of retirement or premature death, and of entitlement to family allowances[12]. In the system for the self-employed there is more concentration — the collecting of the contributions and the payment out of benefits are combined in the same institution, with the exception of health care, sickness and disability benefits, and of part of the pensions and part of the family allowances[13].

Within each branch one can find various institutions with various functions. Putting aside the systems of the self-employed, we find in the employed workers' insurance certain branches where one central institution takes care of all the administrative tasks, and others where more institutions divide the job along various lines. One central institution collects the money from the employers and the employees and divides it between the various other agencies. One central institution deals with the occupational diseases. One agency calculates the old-age and retirement pensions, but another — also central — institution pays them out. More

177

complicated are the branches of illness and disability, unemployment, industrial accidents and family allowances where government agencies co-operate with private institutions of various types[14].

As to the legal position — on top of each branch of social security one finds an undoubtedly public law institution, constituted as a separate entity from the government services and meant to be largely independent from the central government. They have received the very particular name of *parastatale* which expresses their specific nature. They are administered by a board of representatives, half of organisations of employers and half of trade unions. Their budget is separate from the national budget, but they operate under strict control by the government[15].

The administration of the health care, sickness and disability benefits is operated through five national confederations of mutual insurance funds. For unemployment insurance, the paying of the benefits is entrusted to special funds, created by the trade unions. Family allowances are generally paid out by special family allowances funds, created by groups of employers. All these organisations are of a private nature. They existed before the creation of social security and they are authorized by the government to serve under the social security laws.

A special case is found in industrial accidents insurance, which is still managed by private funds and by commercial insurers, who set the premiums and pay out the benefits under an old fashioned compulsory liability insurance legislation[16].

A special feature of the Belgian institutions is the concern with "freedom of choice" of the insured as regards their insurance fund. In all branches where private institutions co-operate for the payment of benefits, the insured can also choose not to use a private fund. For that purpose special public institutions are created which have the same rights and duties as the private funds (including insurance companies for industrial accidents).[17]

B. The Netherlands

The Netherlands have the advantage of a rather well-ordained structure of social security institutions, based upon the division between two branches — the workers' insurance and the general insurance systems. This has not always been so, but it is the fruit of long years of patient reform work[18].

The general insurance laws, creating rights to benefits for all inhabitants, are administered by a central organisational body,

178

with a somewhat surprising structure which we will describe further. The workers' insurance programmes are in the hands of so-called *bedrijfsverenigingen* ("associations of industry"), for each branch of industry. A special case is health care insurance, which is dealt with by a separate institution, the *Ziekenfondsraad* ("sickness funds' council").[19] A special organizational structure also operates for certain unemployment benefits[20].

In the case of workers' insurance, it happens that the same institutions are to perform all the tasks relating to the administration of social insurance legislation: collecting the funds, calculating the benefits and paying them out. In the general insurance systems, the collecting function is separated from the rest and given to the income tax administration. All other functions are assumed by the central administrative body. Only in the health insurance sector is the administration more complicated. The funds are collected partly by the income tax administration, partly by the *bedrijfsvereniging;* the benefits are paid out through a large number of sickness funds of various types; for the so-called "special medical risks" (financed by a general insurance) the benefits can even be paid through commercial insurers.[21].

The legal position of all these institutions is not easy to understand. Especially the administrative organization of the general insurance systems seems strange to the unfamiliar eye. It is composed of a central administrative body, called *Sociale Verzekeringsbank* (which means literally "Social Insurance Bank"), and of decentralised *Raden van Arbeid* ("Labour Councils"). The one is not a bank and the other are not labour councils; they constitute one coordinated body with a central core and decentralized agents[22]. The bank is run by a board of 15 members, one third appointed by organisations of employers, one third by the trade unions and one third by the government. The labour councils consist of a president, appointed by the government and of 6 members, appointed by the minister of social affairs, in the proportion of trade unions for one half and of organisations of employers for the other half. They are clearly institutions of public law operating under strict government control[23].

The *Bedrijfsverenigingen* (associations of industry) of the workers' insurance are considered to be something entirely different, even if they look much the same to the unprejudiced onlooker. They are mandatory associations of employers, according to the branch of industry they are active in. The associations are

179

managed by boards with equal representation of organisations of employers and trade unions. The number of members is not fixed by law, and there is no representative of the government. These associations are considered to be of private law, but they have to be recognized by the government and their decisions can be overturned by the government if contrary to law or to the public interest[24].

Undoubtedly private are the sickness funds and the other insurers who co-operate with the sickness funds council for the administration of health insurance. They can have all types of legal situation and of actual form, and they can be managed in very different ways. The common point is that they have to be recognised by the government, a recognition which will be granted if their statutes comply with "reasonable requirements"[25]. But these agencies have little or no power of decision, they are merely pay-offices for the sickness funds council[26].

C. France

The French legislators have dealt more than any others with the administrative organisation of social security. The result of this long history is a rather simplified system, strongly centralized, in the so-called *régime général,* the social insurance for wage-earners. We will confine our attention to this "general regime", but not without mentioning the existence of various special regimes for particular groups of workers and for the self-employed, who all have their own administrative structures[27]. The result is, of course, a very intricate picture.

Within each regime, and especially within the *régime général* there is specialisation of the institutions according to function. The contributions are collected by an *Agence centrale des organismes de sécurité sociale* ("central agency of social security institutions") through regional offices, called *Unions de recouvrement* ("collecting associations"). For the paying out of benefits there are three national funds, one for family allowances, one for old-age pensions and one for all other risks — illness, disability, industrial accident, occupational disease and premature death (it is called *caisse nationale de l'assurance-maladie,* as if it dealt only with the risk of disease).

The national fund for old-age pensions handles directly the paying of pensions to beneficiaries. The family allowances fund works through 114 local family allowances funds. The National

180

sickness insurance fund covers 16 regional and 122 local funds[28].

All these institutions, including those of the special regimes, are administrated by a board, composed of representatives of the employers and the workers, and, in the regimes for self-employed workers, of representatives of the self-employed. Originally these representatives were elected. With the exception of the agricultural sector these elections have been abolished by the reform of 1967; the representatives are now designated by the organisations of employers and of workers[29]. The reform also introduced the principle of equal representation of workers and employers in all boards, even in those of the *Agence centrale* and the *Unions de recouvrement*, which are, in principle, associations of social security funds[30].

Considering that all these institutions were created by the law; that they had no previous existence; that they are managed in the way ordered by the law; that they cannot legally perform other tasks than these; it becomes very difficult to understand why French experts and the French courts uphold the opinion that they are associations of private law[31]. Also, this opinion is challenged by some of the leading authorities on social law[32].

Only in the field of insurance for self-employed workers and in the agricultural sector is there co-operation of truly private institutions with the social security administration, particularly for agricultural accidents at work and for health insurance of farmers and of other self-employed workers — these risks can be insured with commercial insurance companies under the social security legislation[33]. The original mutual insurance funds *(mutualité)* have been excluded by certain reforms; they deal with private complementary insurance; their only role in the social security context is that of an optional pay-office for the official funds.[34]

D. Germany

In Germany, as in other countries, social insurance has been for a very long time reserved for wage-earners. Only recently has the movement of extension towards the self-employed and other groups become consistent. We will deal mainly with the institutions for wage-earners.

Within the system of social insurance for employed workers — which covers in fact a number of self-employed workers[35] — there is a marked distinction of institutions by risk. Health and disability insurance, old-age, invalidity and survival pensions, industrial accidents and occupational diseases, family allowances and unemployment insurance, all have their own structure.

This structure is a very intricate one[36]. At the one extreme there are family allowances and unemployment benefits, both administered by a central *Bundesanstalt für Arbeit* ("Federal office of labour") and by *Landesarbeitsämter* and 146 *Arbeitsämter* (state and local labour offices). At the other extreme one finds health insurance, managed by nearly 2000 independent health insurance funds, some nationwide, others of only local importance, or limited to the personnel of one firm or the members of one trade. In between there are the structures of pensions insurance and accident insurance. Pensions are administered by 22 pension offices, 18 state offices for ordinary workers, and national offices for railway personnel, for miners, for seamen and for all non-manual workers. Accident insurance is in the hands of 100 insurance carriers, most of which are constituted as *Berufsgenossenschaften* ("occupational associations"), the others being special accident insurance institutions of the local authorities, of the federal government, of the states and of certain fire brigades[37].

Generally, the institutions combine all the functions of social insurance, collecting the premiums, calculating the benefits and paying them out. Certain funds do everything themselves, the others possess a network of regional and local offices[38]. Some institutions delegate part of their job to others. The sickness funds, in particular, do the collecting of the premiums for the old-age, invalidity and survival pensions and for unemployment insurance together with their own.

The legal position of the German institutions causes surprisingly little problem. All authors agree that they are *Körperschaften des öffentlichen Rechts*, which could be translated as "public law corporations"[39]. This is surprising in the first place because there are so many institutions of such different outlook, that one hardly expects them to have a common legal denomination. It is surprising, further, because the French institutions, which are very similar, by and large, to the German, are generally considered as private bodies (see above). It is the more surprising in the case of the *Ersatzkassen* ("replacement funds") who are, in health insurance, the direct descendants of the old *Hilfskassen* ("help funds"), which were undoubtedly private institutions. A recent study discusses possible doubts as to the legal position of these funds, but the conclusion is that they belong to the public law corporations, just like all the other social security institutions[40].

These institutions are characterized by their *Selbstverwaltung* ("self-administration"). This concept covers three elements: (a) financial autonomy — the funds have responsibility for their own financial balance; in health insurance and industrial accidents insurance the funds fix — within certain limits — their own premiums; (b) participation of workers and employers — the general assembly and the board (*Vertreterversammlung* and *Vorstand*) consist of representatives elected by the insured themselves on lists presented by the organisations of employers and the trade unions (it is true that actual elections are rare — the organisations of employers and the trade unions tend to present a common list with just the number of candidates for the position to be won, in which case the election does not take place)[41]; (c) control by the public authorities—the funds are subject to control by the *Bundesversicherungsamt* ("federal insurance office") if their activity extends itself over the territory of more than one state, otherwise the control is done by state insurance offices; the control is of a formal nature; it concerns compliance of the institutions' decisions with their statutes and with the law, and not their merits[42].

E.   Italy

Italy is certainly a special case. On the one hand it offers the picture of true latin proliferation of funds and institutions in an incredible diversity; but on the other hand it may be considered as the European country—on the continent at least—which has most advanced on the way to administrative simplification in social security. Three big administrative institutions cover nearly the whole of the social security business in Italy: the INPS (national institute of social security), the INAM (national institute of health insurance) and the INAIL (national institute of industrial accidents insurance).

Through their regional and local offices, these institutions fulfil all the tasks necessary to administer the social insurance laws, including the collecting of the contributions. The IPNS deals with the risks of invalidity, old age, tuberculosis (for historical reasons treated as a separate risk) and unemployment and it administers the family allowances fund[43]. The INAIL handles the insurance against industrial accidents and occupational disease in industry and agriculture and the INAM provides for

183

health care and sickness benefits insurance[44].

But in fact matters are more complicated. The INPS administers not less than 26 different social insurances, of which most are constituted as separate funds[45]. The INAM was intended to replace the whole multitude of existing funds in health insurance, but in fact many of these funds remained in existence. A decision of the Supreme Court in 1967 declared these funds illegal, but the INAM itself saved their lives by permitting them to administer the health insurance for its account; 22 funds have seized this opportunity[46]. Moreover there are special funds for the health insurance of various groups of civil servants, for farmers and farm workers, for journalists, for artists and for various other categories[47].

The institutions are managed by a president, nominated by the president of the republic, by a board of management with an executive committee, and by provincial committees. These bodies consist of representatives of trade unions, of organisations of employers and of the ministries concerned; there is no equal representation—the trade unions have the majority[48].

For the various special insurances, managed by the INPS, special committees are constituted within the institution. They are generally composed in the same way as the main administering bodies, with representatives of workers, employers and the government, and a majority of the workers[49]. For some special programs there is not a special committee, but a committee of vigilance (*comitato de vigilanza*); it is not clear to what extent the role of such a committee is different from that of a special committee, and in general from the board of management of the institute.

The social security institutions are put under the control of the government. For the special committees and committees of vigilance, this control is effectuated by the board of management of the INPS[50].

F. Conclusions

One can conclude from this rapid overview that there is in fact a large amount of similarity between the systems of administration of social security in continental Europe. Influenced by the early Bismarck legislation in Germany[51] and by the pre-existing workers' mutual insurance funds[52] one finds very generally the social security legislation executed by independent institutions, recognised as incorporated bodies, administered by representatives of the workers' trade unions and of organisations of employers, under the control of the government[53]

The main differences can be summarised as follows:

- election of the representatives in Germany and in the agricultural funds in France, versus designation of the representatives by the unions and organisations in the other countries;
- representation of only the workers and the employers in all administering bodies (Germany, Italy), versus representation of other groups as well, such as the medical profession and family organisations (Belgium, France, Netherlands);
- exceptions from the rule of equal representation of workers and employers; the workers have the majority in Italy, and in the coalminers' funds in Germany;
- direct representation of the government in the administering bodies only in Italy and France, and in the "Social Insurance Bank" and the "Sickness Funds Council" in the Netherlands;
- direct administration of the benefits by public institutions in France, Italy and Germany, versus delegation of part of the work to private operators in Belgium and the Netherlands.

Other striking differences are to be found in the number of institutions, in the criteria of division of the field between the institutions (territorial, by occupation, by risk,) in the legal position of the institutions, in their actual competence, etc. These aspects will be taken into consideration as much as necessary for our further discussion.

The Principles

1. The principle of autonomy of the social security institutions.

When one reads books, articles and reports on the administration of social security in continental Europe, one is forced to admit to a striking unanimity of authors as to a distinction between this administration and that of the central government. Also in the evolution of the legislation the tendency is towards confirmation of separate administration (with increasing government controls) rather than towards a take-over by the central administration of the state, as is the case in Great Britain, the USA and the Scandinavian countries[54].

One of the main reasons for this attitude is merely a traditional

185

one. Social insurance in Europe has for a long time been developed by private institutions, created by workers or by their employers. The people are very much attached to these institutions. When states started to take up the responsibility for the social security of their inhabitants, they conserved as much as possible of the existing structures, in order to benefit from the goodwill and the expertise they possessed[55].

Other arguments have been advanced in profusion, during the long debates that have been held in some countries on the question who would have to administer social security laws. Here are the most important ones:

a. reaction against the tendency of centralisation of all powers in the state administration, as an expression of "state paternalism" or administrative gigantism[56]; this can be expressed as a realisation of the principle of "subsidiarity" of the State, according to which the public authorities should not do what the private associations of citizens can do— a traditional principle of the christian social philosophy[57];

b. increased complication of social legislation and of the situations to which it has to be applied; it is generally alleged that the central government would not be able to deal with all possible cases that can arise; it had better leave this task to independent and specialised institutions who know their field and its problems much more closely[58];

c. financial autonomy—it is often argued that social security should have its own sources of revenue, distinct from the national budget, and that it should be at liberty to use these funds for its own goals; the reverse would be a continuous compromise between social security objectives and other government functions (education, public works, etc.)[59];

d. the insurance principle—some people believe that social security should not only be distinct from the state administration, but that it should remain basically an insurance; the benefits should not be received as a gift from the state, but they should be obtained as a right because of the premiums that have been paid[60]; the benefits should belong to the individual, as "deferred wages" earned by his work[61].

2. The principle of administration by the insured themselves.

The idea of autonomy of the social security systems from the state is, in the minds of many people, linked to that of self-administration. Not only must the social security administration be distinct from the national government, with its own income and its own structures, but it should be in the hands of the insured themselves as payers of the contributions and beneficiaries of the benefits. Practically everybody agrees to this principle in a general way[62].

The motivations for this preference are not always the same. Some people consider it a natural right of those who pay the money to participate in the decisions as to how it will be spent. According to this view the administration of the original social insurance funds in Germany was entrusted by Bismarck to representatives of the employers and the employees, in proportion to their respective share in the contributions[63]. Since the state now pays more or less large subsidies to the social security systems, it should according to the same views, also have its representation in the boards — and in fact this is already partly realised[64]. These views find their strongest expression in the circles of the employers and more particularly in big industry, where they are defended in the name of "responsible management", as opposed to the irresponsible anonymity of the state administration[65].

A very different motivation is that of so-called "social democracy", the right of the people to self-determination. This can be understood as the consistent realization of the principle of subsidiarity of the state (see above)[66]. It can also receive a different meaning, in the eyes of those who understand it as a consequence of the self-responsibility of the people; in that case self-administration is a way of educating the people to responsibility by bringing them to decide by themselves how much money will be spent to social security and who will be eligible for benefits[67].

Still another motivation consists in the concern for flexibility in the development of social security, according to the evolution of the social needs. The administrative structure of the system should be staffed by people who know the real problems by their own experience, and who are likely to find fresh solutions to the new problems that arise, instead of continuing the life of the organization according to Parkinson's law[68]. This can also be seen from another angle; the people should have a knowledge of what goes on in social security, so that a discussion of the problems should take place and that the man in the street should take an interest in it[69].

To these different motivations correspond different ways of realising the self-administration. From our short overview of some continental European systems one will have an idea of this diversity. It is still a very much simplified idea; the actual variation is of such a nature as to defy description[70].

3. The principle of pluralism of institutions.

Less generally accepted is the principle that social security should be managed by competing organisations, working in the same way as commercial firms, except for the profit motive. Advocates of this principle point out that the sting of competition is the only way to keep the organisations alert to keeping administration cost down and to attain the best possible standards of service to the insured[71].

This principle is also adhered to for more philosophical reasons. It is said that the freedom of association is a basic human right; individuals should not be forced to join a given social security organisation if the same objectives can be obtained through freely chosen associations[72]. These reasons may also have a political implication in those countries (Belgium, the Netherlands) where the various "private associations" have certain links with trade unions and with political parties, the free choice of insurance carrier implying an ideologic choice[73].

But the idea of pluralism of private insurance institutions is rejected by many, mainly for reasons of economy, rationalisation and simplification: a concentrated public organisation of the insurance will be able to pay the benefits quicker, at less administrative cost and without unnecessary trouble for the beneficiary who will know where he has to go for his benefits[74].

In fact, the dispute on the question who has to administer social security, the private funds or a public administration, has for a long time overclouded the whole of social security policy in most continental European countries. More has been said on the administrative structures than on the financing, the amount and structure of the benefits and the conditions to obtain them[75].

The Reality

The main point of this paper will be to show how much reality differs from the principles that are put forward, agreed upon or not, as the main principles governing the administration of social security in continental (Western) Europe. The reality I refer to is the legal reality, or the true meaning of the texts and the statutes; I do not intend to make a sociological study of the influences of the government and of several pressure groups upon social security.

Of all the possible points, I will deal only with three: (a) how much power has the government delegated to the social security institutions? (b) who rules the social security institutions? and (c) how much competition is there between the insurance carriers?

I deliberately omit the question of the public or private nature of the insurance institutions, however much importance this debate may have had in several countries[76]. It is my opinion that this question does not affect the reality of the situation, not even from a legal point of view.

(a) *How much power is delegated?*

The degree of autonomy of the social security institutions is, of course, determined by the amount of power the government has delegated to them for the execution of the functions relating to the pursuit of the objectives of the social security system. These functions are manifold and complex, but they can be summarized as follows: fixing and collecting premiums and contributions, establishing entitlement to benefits, calculating benefits, and paying them out. Our question will be: how much of all this has been given to the social security administrative bodies to decide?

The answer must be — not much. The contributions are fixed by the government or by the minister of social affairs as a percentage of the wages or the incomes of the insured; all the elements for the calculation of the contributions are laid down in the law or in regulations. A general exception is the industrial accidents branch, where the contributions are related to risks[77], but even here the elements of the calculation of the premiums are all fixed by the law or regulations[78]. Belgium presents us with the one true exception — industrial accidents insurers can be private associations and even commercial companies, and they can determine freely the insurance premiums to be paid by the employers[79].

Another exception seems to be found in the German health insurance funds, which are free to fix the contributions of the employers and of the workers according to their needs[80]. But this exception is only apparent. The funds see their freedom limited by a legal maximum-limit that can only be exceeded for certain reasons under the control of the federal insurance office[81]. And in fact most or nearly all funds have already reached or exceeded this legal limit[82].

The same can be said for the benefits. Their structure, their amount, the manner of their calculation, the conditions for obtaining them and the procedures to pay them out are all extensively laid down in the laws and regulations. It may be considered as a characteristic of social security legislation, that it wants to regulate everything in detail, leaving little or no freedom for the administering agencies but to apply the regulations[83].

There is a fairly widespread exception, the social insurance funds having the authority to decide on voluntary complementary benefits, possibly financed by way of corresponding voluntary complementary contributions. This concerns in the first place voluntary insurance for basic protection in favour of those groups that are not under compulsory insurance; for instance the health insurance for the elderly in the Netherlands[84] and the industrial accidents insurance of employers in Germany[85]. But for the compulsorily insured also the funds can provide for additional benefits, if additional contributions are paid, for instance in the Italian *assistenza integrativa* and in the German *Mehrleistungen*[86]. It is practically only in France that the funds see their activity confined to the execution of the social security legislation, the complementary insurance being left to private organisations[87].

These complementary benefits do not play an important part in social insurance activity. In Belgium, for instance, the complementary benefits of the health insurance funds, which were to some extent taken by about 90 per cent of the insured, amounted to not more than 3.5 billion BF in 1968, compared to a total of 37.9 billion BF for compulsory insurance[88]. Similar figures, showing even smaller proportions of voluntary benefits, could be given for the other countries.

Even if in Germany the freedom of action of the social insurance funds seems the greatest, we must agree with the *Sozialenquête-Kommission* when it states that "in the activity of insurance carriers the strictly regulated benefits, controlled by the social courts and the collection of the legally fixed contributions are of paramount importance"[89].

The conclusion must be that the social insurance institutions are by no means as autonomous as they seem to be. The fact that the government, either directly or through a special control body, controls the conformity of their decisions to the laws and regulations means that it controls in fact their entire activity, except for a small and relatively unimportant voluntary insurance. It is suggested that the funds should in fact only play a role in the determination of investments for their financial reserves and in the position of their own staff, but even these things are to a large extent regulated by the laws and by government decrèes.

(b) *Who rules the institutions?*

The question who rules the institutions could seem futile after what has been said above. But this is not altogether true. The institutions are not free to collect the premiums and to pay the benefits as they want, but they can apply the legal texts and the regulations in many different ways. For the beneficiary it will make a big difference if the institutions go over every application form and over every piece of proof very carefully, eager to discover or prevent any possibility of abuse, or if they consider it their role to bring the benefits to the insured in the quickest and easiest possible way[90].

The principle is, as we have seen, self-administration. But under no system can there really be administration of the insured themselves. The people on the boards must always be representatives[91]. This problem is the eternal problem of democracy.

The most generally accepted solution is the direct election of representatives. But this brings in a number of problems, apart from those inherent to any system of elections. There is the question of who will vote: must the board represent the insured, the beneficiaries or the payers of the money? The money is generally paid by the workers, the employers and the state; should candidates of the government be presented for the vote of the workers and of the employers? Should, in those systems where the worker does not pay contribution, which is generally so for family allowances, only the employers vote? The workers being much more numerous than the employers, should there be a system of multiple votes for employers? Certain groups of people are beneficiaries without being workers; such people are for instance the husbands or wives of the insured and their dependents[92]; must these people also vote? Similar questions can be asked with regard to the presentation of the candidates.

The French system of election of administrators, as established by the act of 30 October 1946 after a sharp conflict on the "democratic rule" of the funds[93], divides the electorate into two separate groups — employers and workers each vote for their own representatives. All workers, from the age of 18, can vote; employers will have more than one vote if their enterprise exceeds 100 workers. The candidates must present themselves in their own name, they should not be presented by the organizations of employers and of workers, but nothing can stop these organisations from letting the public know who their candidates are. In fact the elections have been a popularity test for the trade unions[94].

In Germany, all social groups who have anything to do with social insurance take part in the voting. All the insured who are at least 18 years old, including the pensioners and, in the agricultural funds, certain self-employed workers can vote[95]. In the coal-miners' funds the vote is indirect, though representatives of the insured[96] which was the old way of electing; for the other funds the election is made in the direct way. But the insured can only choose between lists presented by the organisations of employers, of workers, of pensioners and of self-employed. Groups of insured can also present a free list of candidates, if they find enough people to sign the list[97]. Each group votes for its own representatives; employers have more votes according to the number of their employees[98].

These systems of election have proved a failure. In Germany, where the law provides for this possibility, the elections are generally put aside by the presentation of only one list of candidates. This happened for the most recent elections in all but 52 of the more than 2000 institutions; and in these 52 actual elections, only 20 per cent of the electorate took part in the proceedings[1]. The experience in France was not much better. There was a higher percentage of participation than in Germany; it seems to have been similar to that in the elections for parliament[2] but nevertheless the 1967 reform abolished elections altogether and without very much resistance, representatives in the boards of the various insurance institutions now being simply designated by the "representative" organizations of employers and of workers[3]. By this reform, France has joined the ranks of the other continental European countries where as a rule the boards and committees of the insurance institutions are composed of representatives, designated by the trade unions and the organizations of employers, sometimes also by family organisations and other associations (see above).

This is supposed to constitute a form of democratic rule, the trade unions and the organisations of employers balancing each other out as "social partners" to represent the aspirations of the community in social and economic matters[4]. This apparently widespread belief must, however, be challenged for several reasons:

(a) the employers and workers can represent and balance out their own interest, but not those of the many other groups of beneficiaries, such as students, self-employed, disabled, unemployed, dependent members of the family, etc.[5];

(b) the unions and organizations tend to designate specialists in social insurance matters, who sit on several boards at the same time, becoming more social security administrators than representatives of their groups[6];

(c) there is increasing doubt about the representativeness of these unions and organizations for the whole of the workers and of the employers; especially in the trade unions there is growing concern about the gap between the top and the basis that shows in the sometimes spectacular anti-union strikes of recent years.

In conclusion we must state that there is participation of unions and of organizations but not of the insured themselves[7]. If the aim is self-administration, the structures of social security in continental Europe are a failure.

(c) *Do the institutions compete with each other?*

It is the classical liberal (and neo-liberal) theory that competition is the *conditio sine qua non* for efficiency. Government administration is slow and expensive becuase it holds a monopoly; social security should be administered by independent carriers, competing for the favour of the insured by better service at less administrative cost[8]. At the same time it is argued that this will promote better human relations between the insured and his insurers, it will make the insured feel more responsible towards social security and towards his freely chosen fund and it respects his personal right to choose an institution that corresponds to his own ideological convictions[9].

In reality for the majority of the social insurance funds in Europe there appears to be no choice. The insured belongs *ex lege* to the *Caisse Primaire* of his départment in France[10]; in the Netherlands the employer is automatically affiliated to the *bedrijfsvereniging* ("association of industry") for his branch of activity[11]; also in Germany as a rule the insured is by right a member of the insurance institution for his district, his firm or his occupation[12]. For the Italian insured it is also clear that the insurance relation starts *ope legis* when the insured begins to work in an insured occupation; even if there is some doubt about this automatism for old-age and invalidity pensions, there can be no doubt that the insured is automatically affiliated to a specific fund according to his occupation[13].

In some cases, however, a free choice of insurance carrier remains possible, mainly in the sector of health care and industrial accidents insurance, and sometimes for family allowances and unemployment benefits as well (Belgium). But these exceptions should be seen in their true perspective. In the first place it is not always the insured who makes the choice. Under the Belgian legislation the employer takes an insurance (with a private association or with an insurance company) against the risk of industrial accidents; the worker has nothing to do with it[14]. Similarly, it is the employer who chooses the family allowances fund he wants to affiliate to, the worker having no part in this[15].

In the second place, where there is free choice for the insured himself, this may be very limited. In Germany, especially, the insured can only opt out of his legal health insurance fund into an *Ersatzkasse* recognised for his occupational group (manual workers or non-manual workers) and for his district; the choice is rather limited, there being only 7 *Ersatzkassen* for non-manual and 8 for manual workers[16].

In the third place, insofar as there is real free choice for the insured, the carriers may be much less competitive against each other than one would imagine. The German *Ersatzkassen* have rules, limiting their rights to advertise and to accept new members[17]. The Dutch insured worker can only choose for his health insurance a sickness fund that is recognized for his own district; Mannoury states that there is a tendency to limit the competition between sickness funds at the local level, the insured being generally unaware of any difference between the funds[18]. At any rate, the creation of new sickness funds or the extension of their territory is subject to approval by the Minister of Social Affairs[19]. For Belgian health insurance only the five national confederations of health insurance funds are recognised as insurance carriers (together with an auxiliary fund created by the state); the free choice of the insured is limited to these six institutions, the local funds being only pay-offices, and no new insurance carriers can be admitted under the present law[20]. In a similar way, the free choice under the Belgian unemployment insurance is limited to the three benefit organizations, created by the "most representative" trade unions and to an auxiliary fund, created by the government[21].

So, finally, true competition is only found in the general insurance for special medical care costs in the Netherlands (long term intramural care) and in the Belgian industrial accidents insurance, both being open for private and even commercial insurance associations and companies. This is a situation which some people approve of and want to see generalized[22], but which is deplored by many others, mainly because of the very insecure protection the beneficiary finds in it, and because of the high administrative costs that are in fact the result[23]. An attempt to set up a dual and competing administering structure for sickness benefits and family allowances in the Netherlands had to be given up because of the unwanted effects the spirit of competition produced[24].

Conclusions

The main conclusion of this study is very clear — there is little or no devolution of government power in social security in the Western European continental states[25]. The national parliaments and governments regulate in detail the rights and obligations of all citizens with regard to social security. They only delegate the power to execute the regulations, under their control, to more or less autonomous institutions, generally ruled by representatives of the trade unions and of the employers organizations. Hardly any power is given to specific groups to determine their own contributions and benefits, except as a complementary insurance. No solution is found to the problem of democratic rule in social security, apart from the concentration of power in parliament. The role of private institutions and of competition is marginal and controversial.

No wonder that most experts see the problem of social security administration mainly as a matter of efficacy and expediency[26]. In this respect the most interesting idea has come from the Dutch former minister of social affairs Dr. Veldkamp, who proposes to create a network of "social supermarkets" to modernize the distribution of social security benefits and allied services in the most efficient way to the populations of our countries[27]. And if that happens, nobody will speak any more of social security in colloquia on the devolution of government.

NOTES

1. Pauline Gregg, A social and economic history of Britain, George G. Harrap, London, 6th ed. 1971, p. 180-192.

2. Henri Hatzfeld, Du paupérisme à la sécurité sociale, Paris, Armand Colin, 1971, p. 65-79

3. Erwin Becker, Von der Sozialpolitik zur Sozialreform, Paulus Verlag, Recklingshausen, Sozialkunde heure 4, 1968, p. 39-57.

4. Mr. J. Mannoury, Hoofdtrekken van de sociale verzekering, N. Samsom, Alphen a.d. Rijn, 1967, p. 33-35.

5. Dupeyroux, J.J., Ontwikkeling en tendenties van de stelsels van sociale zekerheid der lid-staten van de Europese Gemeenschappen en Groot Brittannië, Luxemburg, E.G.K.S., 1966, p. 88-109.

6. J. Doublet and J.J. Dupeyroux, Sociale zekerheid in de landen van de E.E.G., Luxemburg, Office of publications of the European Communities, 1962, Social policy series 3, p. 28-29.

7. Jacques Doublet, Droits de l'homme et sécurité sociale, in: Revue Internationale de Sécurité Sociale, Genève, A.I.S.S., 1968, 4, p. 511-524.

8. Mannoury, Dr. J., op. cit.; p. 180; Dupeyroux, J.J., Sécurité sociale, Paris, Dalloz, 2nd ed., 1967, p. 135-137.

9. Mannoury, Dr. J., op. cit., loc. cit.

10. André Van Buggenhout, L'impact macro-économique de la sécurité sociale, Geneva, International Labour Office, 1970, p. 79.

11. Dupeyroux, J.J., Sécurité sociale, p. 138.

12. Herman Lenaerts, Inleiding tot het sociaal recht, Gent-Leuven, Story-Scientia, 1973, pp. 358-72.

13. Herman Lenaerts, op. cit., p. 365.

14. Andre Buttgenbach, Manuel de Droit Administratif, Part II, Brussels 3d ed., 1966, p. 189-218.

15. Buttgenbach, op. cit., p. 188.

16. Paul Anciaux, De arbeidsongevallenwet van 10 April 1971, Huidige stand van de evolutie van de wetgeving op dit gebied, in: Belgisch Tijdschrift voor sociale Zekerheid, 1972, 1, 47-52.

17 Herman Lenaerts, op. cit., p. 382.

18. Veldkamp, G.M.J., De uitvoeringsorganisatie van de sociale zekerheid, in: Social Maandblad Arbeid, Alphen a.d. Rijn, 1974, 4, 235.

19. Mannoury, Dr. J., op. cit., p. 190-191.

20. G.M.J. Veldkamp, op. cit., loc. cit.

21. X., La Sécurité sociale aux Pays-Bas, in: Revue Internationale de Sécurité sociale, 1970, 1, 5-9; Mannoury, Dr. J., op. cit., p. 193-194.

22. L.J.M. de Leede, Het sociale verzekeringsrecht in het administratieve recht, Groningen, Tjeenk Willink, 1973, p. 15.

23. L.J.M. de Leede, op. cit., p. 16; R.A.F. de Guasco, R.H. van der Meer and J.A. Huij, Het sociaal verzekeringsrecht in Nederland, Samsom, Alphen a.d. Rijn, 1971, p. 242-243.

24. L.J.M. de Leede, op. cit., p. 18-19; R.A.F. de Guasco e.a., op. cit., p. 229-232, 237.

25 R.A.F. de Guasco, op. cit., p. 183-184.

26. Dr. J. Mannoury, op. cit., p. 190-191.

27. See for a brief description: Roger Jambu-Merlin, La sécurité sociale, Paris, A. Colin, 1970, p. 52-57.

28. Roger Jambu-Merlin, op. cit., p. 48-51.

29. Roger Jambu-Merlin, op. cit., p. 58-59.

30. Doublet, Jacques, Sécurité sociale, Mise à jour 1969, Paris, Presses Universitaires de France, 1969, p. 37-57.

31. Roger Jambu-Merlin, op. cit., p. 57-58; Dupeyroux, J.J., Sécurité sociale, Paris, Dalloz, 2nd ed., 1967, p. 479-480; Jacques Doublet, Sécurité sociale, Paris, P.U.F., 1967, p. 261.

32. Michel Voirin, Les organes des caisses de sécurité sociale et leurs pouvoirs, Thesis, Paris, 1961; Roger Dillemans, Het statuut van de instellingen der sociale zekerheid in Frankrijk, in: Album Prof. Fernand Van Goethem, Antwerpen, 1964, p. 312-313.

33. Doublet, Jacques, op. cit., p. 386-387.

34. Roger Jambu-Merlin, op. cit., pp. 286-291.

35. Dr. Klaus Gunderjahn, Die Frage des sozialen Versicherungs-schutzes für selbständig Erwerbstätige ... Bonn-Bad Godesberg, 1971, p. 35-42.

36. For a very good discussion of this structure, see: Soziale-enquête-Kommission, Soziale Sicherung in der Bundesrepublik Deutschland, Stuttgart, Kohlhammer, s.d., 101-107.

37. Bundesminister für Arbeit und Sozialordnung, Uebersicht über die soziale Sicherung, Bonn, Bundesministerium für Arbeit und Sozialordnung, 1970, pp. 88, 93, 142, 156-159, 163, 189.

38. Sozialenquête-Kommission, op. cit. p. 102.

39. Bundesminister, op. cit., p. 259; Sozialenquête-Kommission, op. cit., p.104-105;

40. Erich Stolt and Ernst Albert Vesper, Die Ersatzkassen der Krankenversicherung, Bonn-Bad Godesberg, Asgard-Verlag, 1973, p. 52-53.

41. Bundesminister, op. cit., p. 260.

42. Erwin Becker, op. cit., p. 260.

43. Lionello Levi-Sandri, Instituzioni di legislazione sociale, Milano, Giuffré, 1966, p. 55.

44. Id., p. 56-57.

45. Gennaro Ferrari and Giuseppe Lagonegro, Le assicurazioni sociale, Milano, Giuffré, 1971, p. 12-13.

46. M.A. Coppini, Introduction to the complementary systems in Italy, in: European Institute of Social Security, Complementary systems of social security, Part I, Leuven, EISS, 1973, p. 279.

47. For a full description see: Umberto Chiappelli, L'assicurazione sociale di malattia, Giuffré, 1969, 710 p.

48. Lionello Levi-Sandri, op. cit., p. 55-56.

49. Gennaro Ferrari and Giuseppe Lagonegro, op. cit., pp. 171, 185, 197, 212, 222, 236, 253, 264, 278, etc.

50. Gennaro Ferrari and Giuseppe Lagonegro, op. cit., ibidem.

51. Bundesminister... op. cit., p. 259-260

52. J. J. Dupeyroux, Sécurité sociale, p. 139-140.

53. J. Doublet and J. J. Dupeyroux, op. cit., p. 56-65.

54. J. J. Dupeyroux, op. cit., p. 142.

55. J. J. Dupeyroux, Ontwikkeling en tendenties..., p. 173.

56. Erwin Becker, op. cit., p. 45; Henri Hatzfeld, op. cit. p. 161.

57. Erwin Becker, op. cit. p. 31.

58. See e.g.: Wilhelm Frey, Thesen und Anregungen zu einem künftigen System sozialer Sicherung, in: Die Sozialversicherung, 1968, nr. 12, p. 353-357.

59. Doublet, J., Sécurité sociale, p. 347; Eveline Burns, Social Security and public policy, New York, McGraw-Hill, 1956, p. 173.

60. J. Doublet and J. J. Dupeyroux, op. cit., p. 24-25; Lionello Levi-Sandri op. cit., p. 163; W. Klaussen, Kein Verlass auf Vater Staat, Oldenburg, Stalling, 1967, 292.

61. See on this concept the extensive study of Félix Pippi, De la notion de salaire individuel à la notion de salaire social; Paris, Librarie générale de droit et de jirisprudence, 1966, p. 253.

62. Ricardo R. Moles, Aspects administratifs de la sécurité sociale: politiques, problèmes, besoins et perspectives, in: Revue Internationale de Sécurité Sociale, 1973, nr. 3, p. 323.

63. Bundesminister... op cit., p. 259.

64. Herman Lenaerts, op. cit., p. 379-380; J. Doublet and J.J. Dupeyroux, op. cit., p. 64-65.

65. Henri Hatzfeld, op. cit., p. 155-171.

66. Erwin Becker, op. cit., p. 158.

67. Ricardo R. Moles, op. cit., p. 323-324; Henri Hatzfeld, op. cit., p. 88-94.

68. Minister of Social Affairs Claussen (Germany) in: Zeitschrift für Sozialreform, 1974, 4, p. 230-232.

69. Eveline M.Burns, op. cit., p. 263-265.

70. J. Doublet and J. J. Dupeyroux, op. cit., p. 56.

71. Erwin Becker, op. cit., p. 18.

72. Lenaerts, Herman, op. cit., p. 392; Henri Hatzfeld, op. cit., p. 87-94.

73. Roger Dillemans, Handboek van sociale zekerheid, Leuven, Wouters, 1972, p. III. 4; Guy Spitaels, Réflexions sur la politique de sécurité sociale, Brussel, Ed. de l'Universite de Bruxelles, 1973, p. 34-35, Lenaerts, op. cit., p. 382.

74. Herman Lenaerts, op. cit., p. 393-396; Guy Spitaels, loc. cit.; J. J. Dupeyroux, op. cit., p. 138-139.

75. L. J. M. de Leede, op. cit., p. 13; Sozialenquête-Kommission, op. cit., p. 101.

76. Especially in France. See Michel Voirin, op. cit.

77. M. A. Coppini, in European Institute of Social Security, Yearbook 1970, Leuven, the Institute, 1971, p. 543.

78. France: Code de la sécurité sociale, art. 119-121, 132-133 and Décret 31/12/1946, art. 30: Germany: Reichsversicherungs-Ordnung 723-734.

79. Pierre Denis, Droit de la Sécurité Sociale, Brussels, Larcier, 2nd ed., 1973, p. 1J2-114.

80. Bundesminister..., op. cit., p. 140.

81. Reichsversicherungsordnung, 386-391; Kurt Brackmann, Handbuch der Sozialversicherung,Bonn-Bad Godesberg, Asgard Verlag, 1973, p. 364a.

82. Kurt Brackmann, op. cit., ibidem; Sozialenquête-Kommission. op. cit., p. 233-237.

83. Roger Dillemans, op. cit., p. I,16.

84. de Guasco, van der Meer and Huij, op. cit., p. 196.

85. Bundesminister..., op. cit., p. 148.

86. Lionello Levi-Sandri, op. cit., p. 228...; Bundesminister..., op. cit., p. 81 (pensions), 128 (health).

87. Especially the "mutualité", see J. J. Dupeyroux, op. cit., 697...

88. Ministerie van Sociale Voorzorg, Statistisch Jaarboek 1968 van sociale zekerheid, Brussel, Ministry of Social Security, 1970, pp. 212, 292 and 384.

89. Sozialenquête-Kommission, op. cit., p. 105.

90. J. Doublet, op. cit. p. 289.

91. J. J. Dupeyroux, op. cit., p. 139-140.

92. J. Doublet and J. J. Dupeyroux, op. cit., p. 41.

93. J. Doublet, Sécurité sociale, p. 37.38.

94. J. J. Dupeyroux, op. cit., p. 470-472; J. Doublet, op. cit., p. 270-274.

95. Kurt Brackmann, op. cit., p. 155u.

96. Bundesminister, op. cit., p. 260.

97. Kurt Brackmann, op. cit., p. 155wI.

98. Idem, p. 155uV.

1. Statement by Minister of Social Affairs Claussen, in: Zeitxchrift für Sozialreform, 1974, 4, p. 230.

2. J. Doublet, op. cit., p. 272-274.

3. J. Doublet, Sécurité sociale, Mise à jour 1969, p. 37.

4. Eveline M. Burns, op. cit., p. 263-264.

5. Herman Lanaerts, op. cit., 379.

6. eveline M Burns, op. cit., p. 263-264.

7. L. J. M. de Leede, op. cit., p. 19; Sozialenquête-Kommission, op. cit., 105.

8. Erwin Becker, op. cit., p. 18; Henri Hatzfeld, op. cit., p. 33...

9. Herman Lenaerts, op. cit., p. 392-393; Guy Spitaels, op. cit., p. 34-35.

10. J.J. Dupeyroux, op. cit. p. 254-255.

11. Organisatiewet Sociale Verzekering, art. 7; L. J. M. de Leede, op. cit., p. 19.

12. Sozialenquête-Kommission, op. cit., p. 104.

13. Lionello Levi-Sandri, op. cit., p. 193-195.

14. Pierre Denis, op. cit., p. 112-113.

15. Herman Lenaerts, op. cit., p. 393.

16. Erich Stolt and Ernst Albert Vesper, Die Ersatzkassen der Krankenversicherung, Bonn-Bad Godesberg, Asgard, 1973, p. 60-62; Bundesminister op. cit., p. 142.

17. Erich Stolt and Ernst Albert Vesper, op. cit., p. 70-71. Sozialenquête-Kommission, op. cit., p. 106-107.

18. Dr. J. Mannoury, op. cit., p. 193.

19. Ziekenfondswet, art. 34.

20. Act of 9th August 1963, art. 3-5; Pierre Denis, op. cit., p. 204.

21. Pierre Denis, op. cit., p. 201.

22. For instance H. L. Kunneman, Bleidooi voor een decentralisatie van de gezondheidszorg, Leiven, Batteljee en Terpstra, 1970, p. 54.

23. Guy Spitaels, op. cit., p. 34-35; J. J. Dupeyroux, op. cit., p. 137-138; J. Mannoury, op. cit., p. 193-194.

24. Dr. J. Mannoury, op. cit., p. 181.

25. It may be interesting to observe that there is also no upward devolution toward supranational bodies, such as the E.E.C. See on this subject: J. J. Ribas, La politique sociale des Communautés Européennes, Paris, Dalloz et Sirey, 1969, p. 411; J. Van Langendonck, De harmonisering van de sociale zekerheid in de E.E.G., Leuven, Rechtsfakulteit, 1971, p. 116.

26. J. J. Dupeyroux, op. cit., p. 135-136; Sozialenquête-Kommission, op. cit., p. 101; Herman Lenaerts, op. cit., p. 393-394; Paul O'Higgins, Efficacité des structures administratives, in: European Institute of Social Security, Yearbook 1970, Leuven, the Institute, 1971, p. 351-355.

27. G. M. J. Veldkamp, De uitvoeringsorganisatie van de sociale verzekering, in: Sociaal Maandblad Arbeid, 1974, 4, p. 239; Guy Spitaels, op. cit., p. 37.